WHY WE REMAIN JEWS

WHY WE REMAIN JEWS

The Path to Faith

VLADIMIR TSESIS, MD

ACADEMY CHICAGO PUBLISHERS

Published in 2013 by
Academy Chicago Publishers
363 West Erie Street
Chicago, Illinois 60654

© 2013 by Vladimir Tsesis

First edition.

Printed and bound in the U.S.A.

Library of Congress Cataloging-in-Publication Data

Tsesis, Vladimir.
Why we remain Jews : the path to faith /
Vladimir Tsesis. — First edition.
volumes cm
Includes bibliographical references.
ISBN 978-0-89733-732-8 — ISBN 978-0-89733-717-5
1. Jews—Identity. 2. Faith. 3. Judaism and science.
4. Tsesis, Vladimir. I. Title.
DS143.T77 2013
305.892'4077311092—dc23
[B]
2013015968

TABLE OF CONTENTS

To my grandchildren,
Ruthie and Ariel,
who are my future.

ACKNOWLEDGMENTS

FIRST OF ALL I am most grateful to my wonderful wife, Marina, who is always my best friend, adviser, and inspiration. She and my son Alexander were my main source of encouragement for writing this book.

I am deeply indebted to Laura De Santo Wagner, who did an excellent job as an editor of the manuscript before it was submitted to the publisher.

By a stroke of destiny I met Eric Miller at the right place and the right time. He was the first to read the entire manuscript when it was ready to be sent to prospective publishers and deemed it worthy to be presented to a wide audience. I am very grateful to him for his friendliness and unfailing optimism.

My deep gratitude to the wonderful folks at Academy Chicago Publishers; Zhanna Vaynberg and Genevieve Salazar, who both helped me form my manuscript into a finished work, and co-founders Jordan and Anita Miller, who decided to take a chance with me.

"My father is Jewish, my mother is Jewish, I am Jewish."
—Daniel Pearl, 2002. Last words before he was murdered by militants in Pakistan

"There are two ways to live your life. One is as though nothing is a miracle. The other is as though everything is a miracle."
—Albert Einstein

"The unexamined life is not worth living."
—Socrates

INTRODUCTION

THE IDEA OF CREATING THIS BOOK occurred to me when one of my close friends suggested that I write a story explaining how I came to my belief in God. I gladly accepted the proposal to express my thoughts about the Divine Presence, because, though I was brought up by parents who were skeptical about religion and even God's existence, the idea of God has never left me since I was a young child.

I started to write a short story, but soon I realized that the concept of faith in God is very broad. It does not exist in abstract reflections but is a result of numerous events, meetings, thoughts, observations—everything that is called life.

Indeed, in order to describe and understand the path an individual has taken to God, it is necessary to tell where he grew up, who his parents were, what important people he encountered during his lifetime. . . Besides this, there is also the inherent and individually unique evolution of views on the different aspects of existence that serve as a foundation of our encounters with Him who gave us the gift of conscious life.

It took me two years to fulfill my friend's request and present this story, in which I share with my reader events, meetings, and ideas that have led me to a firm belief in God.

The title of this book was inspired by a lecture titled, "Why We Remain Jews, or Can Jewish Faith Still Speak to Us?" by the late political professor, classicist and Jewish thinker Leo Strauss given to a small audience at the Hillel Foundation at the University of Chicago in February 1962. In my book, I want to give the reader a sense that faith is not a whim of the imagination, caprice of thought, or "the opium of the people."

Religion, in my view, is the only option available to us that allows an honest, logical, and appropriate response to the resolution of the innermost secrets of human existence. For me, such a conclusion is based—among other reasons—on the abysmally short life of human beings in comparison with the age of the universe they live in, on the facts of human history, and on the whole human experience that accompanies us during the limited time of our lives.

This book has been written by a Jew, and, naturally, it tells the story of Jewish self-identity and of Judaism. However, it might be of interest to anyone searching for Truth.

I believe in one of the fundamental doctrines of my religion, which is paraphrased in the American Declaration of Independence: ". . . that all men are created equal, that they are endowed by their creator with certain unalienable Rights, that among these are Life, Liberty and the pursuit of Happiness." In other words, following what is written in the Torah, because all men are created in the divine image and likeness, each human being is equally entitled to be respected by other people.

Judaism is the family in which I was born and raised, and it is inseparable from the core of my personality.

Following one of the basic tenets of Judaism, I believe that the righteous—not only Jewish people, but everyone who in life performs virtuous deeds—can equally count on the reward of the Almighty after death.

Introduction

In this book, I tell true stories about my life experiences that have formed my ideas about God and religion.

People generally follow, in varying degrees of balance, both their rational consciousness and the voice of their hearts. To those for whom the voice of the heart is not enough to bring them to faith in God, I tell them, contrary to popular opinion, religion and science are not antagonistic but complementary to each other, each fulfilling the function assigned to it in humanity's perception of the world. Moreover, it is my firm conviction that, when examined without prejudice, religion and science are in perfect harmony. In order to support this view (which may seem inconsistent to some readers) I rely on the objective evidence of the latest achievements of advanced scientific thinking.

The concept of being Jewish has a religious, a cultural, and an ethnic component. Therefore, in this book, these perspectives always go hand in hand.

Another reason I had for writing this book was the desire to share my own experience of taking the first steps and then becoming fully involved in the life of the synagogue and the Jewish community.

I hope that those readers who are attracted by my invitation to continue the glorious religious tradition of their fathers will, like me, find a deep psychological satisfaction in a pure, not politicized, faith in God, in the covenants of His Torah, and in an active involvement in the religious life of His people.

DENYING GOD

MANY ENLIGHTENED acquaintances of mine often wonder why I—"an educated person"—believe so strongly in God. Before giving an answer to such a question I ask my companions to explain what *prevents* them from believing in God. Their responses vary widely. Some of them flatly reject religion; others keep a mysterious silence or shrug their shoulders.

I am not at all surprised by the reactions of atheists, who reject God's existence out of hand and completely. Indeed, we live in a free country where everyone has a right to hold his own views. Much more amazing to me are the responses of those who might be called skeptics. These are the people who wonder why others believe in God, but at the same time never miss an opportunity to hold religious ceremonies: to celebrate the B'nei Mitzvah of their children, weddings, and the births of babies in their families. Moreover, they show even more respect for religious traditions when they go through trying times. During religious ceremonies, such people always demonstrate their sincere respect for worship and the sermons delivered by rabbis.

It seems to me that these people—on the one hand ignoring religion, and on the other hand professing it—are so busy and involved in the maelstrom of life that, in the daily bustle of reality, they have no time to stop for a minute and realize that "man shall not live by bread alone." (Deuteronomy 8: 2–3).

There is a religious school affiliated with the synagogue where I have been attending services for many years. Children come to this school two or three times a week. As a rule, they are brought there by their parents.

On Sundays, the school time coincides with the morning worship—*Shaharit*. This service is not long. Since the children are attending religious school, surely, it could be assumed that their parents want them in the future to be religiously educated Jews. Naturally, one is led to think that such parents would be glad to attend the religious service themselves.

However, these parents are very seldom willing to use this ideal opportunity to set a good example for their children. Instead of joining the service, they demonstrate their lack of interest in religion. While the children are getting religious lessons, some of the parents go home or run errands; others stay in the synagogue whiling away the time in different ways—talking with one another, making phone calls, reading books and newspapers.

I have often wanted to ask them one question: why do they bring their children to a religious school if they themselves are obviously not interested in practicing their religion? And, really, are they so naïve that they fail to understand that their children are not stupid, that they see and are influenced by the inconsistent behavior of their beloved parents?

But there is always room for optimism. Some people will always find their way to God, especially if they are exposed to religious values in their childhood.

* * *

My parents were born before the Great October Revolution in Russia and grew up in families where Jewish traditions were observed; they were about ten years old when Lenin's party came to power. Like most people of that time, having suffered the bloody turbulence of revolutionary turmoil, my parents, especially my mother, desperately wanted to adapt to the new lifestyle in order to survive under the new political system.

During the post-revolutionary years, the Soviet government persecuted religious adherents and stifled and suppressed religion by any means available, doing its utmost to connect the idea of God with negative associations.

In order to avoid the risk of disappearing as a result of regular purges, as happened to many people at that time, my parents had no choice but to conceal their religious views.

Gradually, a strange phenomenon that was typical in that period occurred: the more they distanced themselves from religion, the more positively they accepted the views imposed on them by Soviet antireligious propaganda. Eventually, they began to identify themselves with those who continually brainwashed them into believing that the religion of their fathers and mothers was nothing more than a reprehensible, ignorant superstition.

My paternal grandfather was a *melamed*—a religions teacher, and my maternal grandfather was a cantor and a *shohet*—a ritual slaughterer. Both were killed by German fascists and their local accomplices during the war, so I never had a chance to meet them.

When I asked my father—a communist by necessity— why he refused even to consider the possibility of the existence of God, he told me that it was a result of his life experience. He said that his family was very poor, so to help his parents to make ends meet he had had to work from an early age. One of his jobs was at a coaching inn, where he was an errand boy. There he repeatedly observed priests who came into town from surrounding villages and who were among the most active customers of the local prostitutes. For the rest of his life my father believed that behind the outward holiness of the clergy lurked hypocrisy and deceit.

"How can somebody be religious," he told me, "if the so-called 'holy men' behave worse than the ungodly? What is a religion when there's nothing holy in its holy orders?"

While he was trying to avoid giving me a direct answer, my father could see by the expression on my face that the trivial generalization gathered from his own life experience failed to convince me. After a pause, he continued much more gravely:

"Look, Vovka. I went through the war from the first to the last day, I fought with Germans, many of my friends and fellows were wounded or killed before my eyes. There were times when I met death daily. When you grow up, you will realize that, after going through all that, it was difficult for me to even think about God, to say nothing of talking about Him. Do you understand me? My God is my family, the future of my children, that's all. And let's not discuss the rest, OK?"

THERE ARE NO ATHEISTS
IN FOXHOLES

WHEN I THINK ABOUT the ambivalent position of many people toward religion, I always remember Sheldon and Gretchen Weisberg, whom I knew for many years.

Sheldon Weisberg was fifteen years older than I was. For many years he was my neighbor in the locker room of the fitness club that we and our wives attended. Prior to retirement, Sheldon had spent many years working as a high-level administrator in the Chicago school system. Because Sheldon was, among other things, an inveterate Jewish liberal, the number of topics we could discuss was not very large. Initially, we talked about—and quickly exhausted—neutral subjects like geography, climate, and the food and customs of Ukraine, where Sheldon's ancestors came from.

Our limited regular dialogue had reached a deadlock when Sheldon, in a solemn manner, revealed to me how incredibly fond he was of communist-era Russia.

He had grown up in a family of American Jewish Communists and imbibed a strong faith in communism with his mother's milk. One summer, when he was already a young man, during his regular visit to a communist camp in Wisconsin Sheldon met his future wife Gretchen, a daughter of non-Jewish German communists.

After they were married, their burning passion for the dictatorship of the victorious proletariat inspired Sheldon and Gretchen to pay three "goodwill visits" to Russia during the "blessed" Stalinist time.

In the Mercedes they acquired in post-war West Germany (not in the communist East Germany), the Weisberg couple drove around Moscow, Leningrad, Minsk, and Kiev.

Communist paradise made an indelible, vivid impression on them.

As a result, all my attempts to tell them the true story about the Soviet Union as an eyewitness, were, at best, met with a patronizing smile, and, at worst, with the unconcealed irritation of idealists whose Utopian ideas should be off limits to discussion. Sheldon countered my arguments with an undisguised sense of moral superiority, reproaching me that, during my more than thirty years in the Soviet Union, I could not realize what a wonderful country I lived in, something he and Gretchen had easily grasped during their short visits. The couple was in love with communism while happily enjoying all the benefits of capitalism.

Later, Sheldon became irritated with my attitude toward the political situation in the Middle East, my opinion on the right to self-defense, my views on the rights of parents to send their children to the schools of their choice, and my thoughts on many other subjects. His anger reached the highest level when I told him that I believe in "comrade" Darwin's Theory of Evolution much less than I believe in God, the Author of the Universe. Hearing this kind of "rebellious thought," Sheldon did not conceal his righteous indignation; for some reason, atheists feel as if the ground is slipping from under their feet when they are told that they, as well as the rest of the human race, are not descended from monkeys but were created according to God's will.

Sheldon remained a pure altruist as long as people accepted his "expert" opinion.

Since Sheldon could not forgive me the political incorrectness I had demonstrated on so many occasions, our relations gradually became limited to the formal exchange of greetings. But we still lived in the same neighborhood and would run into each other in different places.

Once, my wife, Marina, and I met Sheldon and Gretchen in a local restaurant. We greeted one other, and then Sheldon and Gretchen invited us to their table. This invitation was hard to refuse, so we joined them. Being aware of the pro-Soviet sentiments of our neighbors, Marina and I did our best to avoid subjects associated with Russia. However, soon Gretchen and Sheldon started singing the praises of the Soviet system—which by this time had been firmly buried in history—clearly letting us know the position that we "reactionaries" held was hopelessly immoral because it rejected the essence of communist virtues.

I wanted to stay silent, but I could not help reminding the enthusiastic couple that the Soviet system they adored so much had cost Russia millions of innocent lives.

Sheldon and Gretchen, though, were not impressed in the least with the staggering number of victims of Soviet communism—for them, the eventual achievement of communism's great ends justified all means.

Trying to avoid conflict, I decided not to express what I thought about the Weisbergs' offensive attitudes towards the Soviet experiment. Somehow I changed the subject, shifting to neutral topics. Then it was time to say goodbye.

"Whatever your response may be, Vladimir, I just have to share my opinion with you," Gretchen said at parting. An insidious smile on her face promised that the next moment I would hear something quite unpleasant. Then, all-knowingly, with an air of moral superiority, she continued loudly, so that everyone in the dining room could hear.

"You can say whatever you want, but if it wasn't for your beloved America, Soviet Russia would still flourish and prosper to the joy of progressive mankind! The magnificent experiment of communist Russia was ruined by no one else but your beloved American government. That's it!"

"Having such a disposition," I retorted, "why didn't you both apply for political asylum in your beloved Russia a long time ago, so you would be able to participate in building the society of your dreams? In Russia, they would be more than happy to provide you with a communal apartment, where you would share your kitchen and toilet with five or six other proletarian families and where you would never have hot water, and rarely even cold water, coming out of your communal faucet. They would give you a job and you would get a salary, which would prevent you from starving and pay for most urgent needs, but would not be enough for anything else."

That should have been the end of our relationship, but we still had mutual acquaintances: childhood friends of the Weisbergs and members of our synagogue, Leah and Arnold Levenson. Leah became ill with a serious kidney disease, and, after several years of dialysis, passed away at the age of seventy. Leah's *yahrzeit*—the Jewish religious memorial service—held at the Levenson's residence, was attended by almost the entire congregation, including the rabbi and the cantor. Naturally, best friends of the Levensons—Sheldon and Gretchen—were there as well. When the rabbi started the worship service, Gretchen excused herself and went to help in the kitchen, while Sheldon remained in the room.

During the reading of the Mourners' Kaddish, following the ancient tradition, everyone who came to pay their last respects to Leah was standing facing East, holding the booklets specially printed for the occasion and saying the prayers that Jews have said from time immemorial. Only Sheldon did not pray. Sheldon was eloquently demonstrating that he just happened to be present at this ceremony but that it was totally alien to him. A person standing next to Sheldon tried to be helpful by offering him his own booklet, but Sheldon proudly rejected it with an abrupt negative shake of his head.

Well, I thought, Sheldon has every right to pray or not to pray. What looked quite annoying was not so much his demonstrative refusal to participate in the communal service as his ironic arrogant glances at everyone who did not share his atheism. I hoped that Sheldon—at least for the sake of appearances—would join in saying the word "Amen" in memory of the person who had been quite close to him, but he did not do even that.

After Leah's *yahrzeit*, our greetings were reduced to a slight nod for some time, until one day I again met Sheldon in the locker room. On his face, instead of his characteristic expression of complacency, was a look of anxiety and worry. At that time he apparently needed to share his current problem with anybody, because he said hello to me in a much friendlier way than usual. Thus, for the lack of anyone more suitable, I became his confidant.

"What's new?" I couldn't help but ask Sheldon, responding to his invitation to talk.

"You see, Vladimir," he said without any preliminaries, "I developed cataracts in both eyes, for which I recently had surgery. The cataracts were removed, but—can you imagine?—during the operation the ophthalmologist touched something in my right eye, and, apparently because of this, now I have a strange small spot in my field of vision.

"This disturbs me a lot, but I can't get rid of it. The doctor examined me twice; he told me that it should pass, but he's not a hundred percent sure. And you, as a physician, what do you think about this?"

"You know, Sheldon, I'm a pediatrician, not an eye doctor," I answered, "but I think that your doctor has no reason to lie to you. Your problem, indeed, should pass by itself."

Sheldon liked my answer. Immediately regaining his natural dignity, he asked me with a smile:

"Do you really think so?"

"I am sure, Sheldon," I replied. "No doubt. With God's help, everything should be okay."

"Yes. With God's help, I hope. I feel better already," Sheldon automatically continued with enthusiasm, then suddenly stopped short, blushing heavily. No wonder: he had given himself away completely. It turned out that atheist Sheldon "could not care less" for God, until it came to his personal health.

Two years later, on a Sunday morning, I sat at a table in the local coffee house which was frequented by the Weisbergs, who lived nearby.

I had hardly begun eating my breakfast, when suddenly, right in front of me, I noticed Sheldon. He was alone; his shoulders were hunched. His face expressed bitterness and pain. We exchanged greetings, and I asked him why he had come without Gretchen.

"Oh, Gretchen is in the hospital," Sheldon responded mournfully.

"What's the matter with her?"

"Leukemia. She got sick a couple of weeks ago and now she is in the hospital. . . More than a week. . ."

"What kind of leukemia?"

"Oh, don't even ask. A very bad form. It's a myeloid leukemia. But doctors say that sooner or later she should go into a remission. Let's hope so. . ."

Fully realizing that, considering the ominous diagnosis and the quick progression of symptoms, Gretchen's prospects were far from optimistic, I offered my sincere sympathy. There could be no doubt that Sheldon would soon undergo many severe emotional trials concerning his wife's health.

In response to my good wishes, Gretchen's husband only energetically nodded, and, at a brisk pace for a man of his age, went toward the exit.

Unfortunately, he was faced with the inevitable prosaic reality of life—in this case the illness of his beloved wife.

Arnold Levenson, Sheldon's friend, was a regular member of the morning *minyan* at our synagogue, and from time to time I asked him about Gretchen's health. One morning, shortly after the celebration of Chanukah, when the religious service was over, Arnold and I had a cup of coffee.

At that time Gretchen had been ill for more than two months. After talking about this and that, I asked Arnold about the Weisbergs. Though he had been friends with the Weisbergs for many years, Arnold, being a moderate liberal, did not share their fellow-travelers ideas; he openly and good-naturedly made fun of their ridiculous revolutionary demagoguery. Arnold also had a gift that I have noticed in not too many people—the ability to speak about the most tragic things with a knowing smile. That "smile through the tears" was supposed to mean: "Nothing can be done. Such is life. Enjoy it while you can. . ."

"So how are things with Gretchen?" I asked him.

"How are things with Gretchen?" he repeated after me. "Bad enough. She's been at home for a month now. She does not feel well, but doesn't complain. This, of course, has drastically transformed Sheldon's life. Before this he was treated like a king by Gretchen. She used to do all the housework, and now he has to look after everything."

"What do the doctors say about Gretchen's prognosis? Is she bedridden, or can she walk?" I asked.

"Well, she looks after herself quite well. Next week she will have to undergo another traumatic procedure: a bone marrow biopsy. But she gives no sign that she is worried, and, not only that, she is the one who comforts Sheldon. Gretchen is an incredible woman—right now she is doing all she can for Sheldon to free him from the chores that will need to be done when she dies. She doesn't want him to feel lonely in the future. . ."

"What is *her* mood?"

"Oh, she's a real heroine. Gretchen doesn't give up. She just did something I would never expect of her. Recently I went for a visit, and, to my surprise, I saw her standing by the table and lighting candles on a shining tall Chanukiyah. I never would have dreamt I would find such an object in the home of those ardent atheists. And that wasn't all. What do you think this German woman was doing? She was lighting the next Chanukah candle and reading a blessing in Hebrew transliterated into English from a piece of paper. I couldn't resist asking her what she was doing!

"And you know what? She looked at me intently and replied as if she was offended by my inappropriate question: 'What is so strange about it, Arnold? Shouldn't you light candles during Chanukah?'

"I was really shocked. Chanukah candles in the home of such militant atheists as the Weisbergs?! Who would imagine that!"

"Come on, Arnold," I interrupted him, "are you pulling my leg? It is absolutely impossible! Gretchen is a staunch daughter of German communists and an even more confirmed atheist than her husband, and suddenly she's observing a Jewish ritual that is completely foreign to her nature and upbringing? No way!"

Oh, what a dirty look Arnold gave me! His glance revealed an indulgent regret for my naïveté. "Just look how incredulous you are! And what would you say if I told you that she made her honorable husband, the American almost-communist, buy the best silver Chanukiyah at the Rosenblum store in West Rogers Park? Would you believe that?"

Though Arnold was telling me all these things, I still was not able to understand what a human being is capable of, as he understood it. I still could not see through his eyes.

A smile, directly proportional to the degree of intended irony, appeared on his round face. Pointing his fleshy finger at me, he took another loud gulp of coffee and said, "As long as I could remember, Gretchen had said she wanted to be cremated after death. Now she has let Sheldon know that she wants to be buried in a coffin by a Jewish funeral home in a

Jewish cemetery. She has ordered the coffin herself and paid extra in order to have the coffin lid adorned with a big Star of David."

"But Gretchen is not even Jewish," I said. "Why should she need all that!"

"Ah, Vladimir. What do you know about people? You know nothing! Let me tell you and you just listen." Arnold's walrus-like face cracked into a wide smile. "I have known the Weisbergs for many years. Whenever they went on different tours, wherever they traveled, they never missed the opportunity to visit notable synagogues all over the world, although they were indifferent to churches.

"You've never been to their home, have you? As for me, I'm at home there. They have all the walls of their living room covered with pictures, not of people, not of landscapes, not of animals or flowers, but of the synagogues they have visited. And that's all."

Arnold got up to leave, and there was nothing left for me to do but to recall a wise saying: "There are no atheists in foxholes."

THE IDEOLOGY OF
SELF-PRESERVATION

MY MOTHER GREW UP not far from Proskurov in Galicia, now the city of Khmelnitsky, in a small Jewish *shtetl* (township) called Tcherny Ostrov. In the early years of the Russian Revolution, that area was a crossroads for the movement of various gangs, none of which missed the opportunity to inflict another pogrom.

One day the *shtetl* was "visited" by Symon Petliura's band. Anticipating another big pogrom, the local Jews gathered in the synagogue and barricaded its doors and windows. In the evening, when Petliura's thugs started to shoot blindly through the windows at the Jews who were trying to save themselves, everybody dropped to the floor and lay side by side.

Under the ominous sounds of shooting, my mother, twelve years old, tightly hugging her best friend, lay in complete darkness. Suddenly, her friend cried out loudly and then fell silent.

For the rest of her life, my mother never forgot that horror: her dress was soaked through with what not long before had been the brain of her best friend. The dead girl was still tightly clutching my mother's hand.

This and many similar tragic episodes left my mother with deep psychic traumas.

She could never forget the pogroms of her childhood and the subsequent social persecution and discrimination she underwent during the first years of the Soviet regime— because, in the eyes of the new ruling class, she was considered a disloyal, religious, petit bourgeois element.

The new revolutionary class, ideologically insisting upon its historical predestination, appropriated unlimited rights to use relentless violence against the social classes it disliked and anyone who disagreed with them.

My father moved to another city from the place he grew up and wrote on his identity papers that he came from the poor family of a common craftsman, instead of a religious teacher of Judaism. This was believable and allowed him to belong to a social class that was loyal to the new regime. In a short time he became a Komsomol member and a Komsomol organizer.

With a Komsomol mission, he arrived in Tcherny Ostrov, where he met and married my mother. Because of this marriage, the local communist activists stopped ostracizing my mother and forever forgot her previous social status.

After many years of stress, and bombarded by the tireless propaganda of the new society, my mother came to believe in atheism, subconsciously convincing herself of the absence of divine power in her life, though she continued for the rest of her life to remember many words from the prayers and songs of religious services.

She lost her faith in God for the same reason almost all of her generation did: survival at any cost became vital in a country controlled by the dictatorship of the proletariat.

When I was a child, I would ask my parents the meaning of the word "God." I always got the same reaction. "Why don't you keep those questions to yourself? A child like you cannot understand these things. People strive every day to survive and put a piece of bread on the table for their family, and you trouble us with your stupid questions about God!"

"UNHEALTHY" CURIOSITY

EXPLAINING THE EMOTIONAL NEED of human beings to believe in God, Blaise Pascal, the famous French mathematician and physicist, said, "The heart has its reasons, which reason does not know." Most people either inherit their faith in God from their parents or absorb it from the environment they grow up in. But if they live in surroundings where God's name is seldom mentioned, their belief in God becomes the result of a deep inner motivation and unconscious impulses emanating from the human heart, which tries to find meaning in the world where it exists.

Meeting in different countries around the world with young people from the former Soviet Union who have chosen the Orthodox Jewish lifestyle, I have asked them time and time again what exactly made them break away from their conventional lives, from the norms of the secular society they had been familiar with from childhood; what led them to a religious way of life that required much more self-discipline and resistance to the numerous strong temptations of modern society.

To this question I would hear a variety of answers, but not even once did I hear that it was some magical word, comment, or event that had prompted them to follow a religious path. That led me to think that in most cases people decided to observe the centuries-old Jewish traditions for the rest of their lives not because of some special turning point, but because they needed to fill a spiritual void. Living in a democratic society, where they had an opportunity to exercise their free will, they came to this decision following the voice of their own hearts and souls.

The same impulses have been responsible for my own gradual coming into religion. When I was young, many adults thought I was a strange child because of my "unhealthy" curiosity. "What kind of a son do you have?" they would ask my parents in Yiddish. "Other children act like children, while he is interested in strange, useless nonsense. Is he sick or what? Why, instead of asking about things that make sense, does he want to know about the purpose of life? Is he a *bisele mishuge*, *Got zol upitn* (a little crazy, God forbid)?"

And, indeed, I never ceased to wonder why human beings, including myself, were given the gift of life. To my questions about the purpose of existence, adults first answered with a sympathetic and understanding smile—as if I suffered from some inherent mental defect—and then politely, but firmly, told me not to disturb them with "such stupid questions" in the future.

"Why stupid?" I would object. "Not stupid at all. After all, are we all born to live only to then die once and for all? There is no exception for anyone. Why is life given to a man? To be born, to get one's fill, and then to die?"

"Look at him! He is asking 'why'? Did you forget about children, smart aleck? We all live for our children. Is it so difficult for you to understand, boy?"

"But in that case, for example, what do childless people live for?"

"Velvl (my name in Yiddish), people live to contribute to progress, so that those who live after them can use what they have created and remember them for their good deeds."

"Yes, but all the people who have died, those whom we knew well, they were quite ordinary and did not create anything special in their lives. Their only concern while they were alive was providing enough food to support their families. These people who had children or were childless, some good and some not so good, they are remembered by their families and friends for a relatively short time after their death—for months or for years. But with time, the memories left by them become more and more vague, and, eventually, the people are completely forgotten. So, please, answer me at least one question: why did these people live, labor, go to work? What is the purpose of my life and of yours?"

I asked this kind of sincere question only of those adults who I believed were equipped with a solid measure of worldly wisdom.

Sooner or later, these people started to avoid me in different ways, first politely and then by requesting me to leave them alone. They let me know that, instead of pestering them with what they called "silly, stupid questions," I should busy myself with useful things.

Like the inquisitive children of preceding generations, I did not ever get satisfactory answers to the most important questions of existence. Fortunately, there were books, where I found some possible answers to what I was interested in. Thus, little by little, books became my best friends.

FACING THE HOLOCAUST

DURING MY CHILDHOOD YEARS, my sense of belonging to the Jewish people was based on nationality and ethnic origin rather than religion. This was how the overwhelming majority of my Jewish peers felt, too.

At an early age, I heard of the tragic fate that befell the Jewish people during World War II. At first I learned from my mother that more than thirty members of her family of all ages living in Tcherny Ostrov were killed by Germans and local Ukrainian policemen. My mother occasionally shared her grief with me, but I, as a typical child, did not want to think beyond my happy, carefree existence to days consisting of horror and nightmare. As I never knew any of our murdered relatives, the barbaric brutality my mother had described appeared rather abstract and unreal to me. That went on until my innate optimism was crushed. In 1951—I was ten at that time—my father brought home a tattered book without a cover and with pages torn from both ends, which he had found who knows where. Silently, he opened it to a specific page, put it in front of me on the table as I did my homework, and, without saying a word, left the room.

Curious, I glanced at the title of a story on the opened page: "The Hell of Treblinka." It was an article by the famous Soviet writer Vasily Grossman, an account of what he had witnessed in 1945, as a war reporter, when, along with the Soviet troops, he entered the Treblinka death camp, a factory for the annihilation of Jews of all ages. This essay contained all the information necessary for people all over the world with normal morals and integrity to appreciate the degree of unheard-of atrocities inflicted on the Jewish people by the Nazi ideology in action.

Forgetting everything else around me, I read a harrowing indictment condemning humanity for allowing, in an inconceivably short time, the unthinkable destruction of the fundamental laws of human ethics and morality. What I learned made me years older, once and for all shutting behind me the door to my happy childhood.

In that post-war period, it was not customary for parents to ask children about their feelings and thoughts. For several weeks, I had the sensation that a terrible, monstrous hole had opened in my heart: in this world, where as a child I enjoyed many cheerful smiles and kind words, it turns out there also existed a huge number of people capable of infinite evil. My whole childish being was outraged by something I could not imagine as belonging to the human race.

Several times I tried to discuss this subject with my father, but, unable to answer my questions, he avoided conversations of that kind. Only on one occasion was I able to "drive him into a corner." During this episode, initially, he did his best to explain to me what I was asking, but he very soon gave up his effort, faltered, and, looking into the distance, only embraced me tenderly, stroking my head. He, who participated in combat operations during the war against fascism, was at a loss for words to explain to me why people could behave more violently and cruelly than predatory animals.

It was not only the scope of the tragedy of the Holocaust that was the source of my moral anguish. I was also frustrated by the consciousness of the fact that even the catastrophe which had befallen my people, even such an enormous evil, had not made the world better, had not taught the people of the world to treat one another with respect, sympathy, and understanding.

A schoolmate who lived near my house had a neighbor, an eighteen-year-old Jewish girl called Zoya. Having nobody else to turn to, I decided to discuss my deep emotional trauma with her. Her eyes wide, she attentively listened to me, and when I paused, she went to the bookcase and pulled out carefully hidden, typewritten sheets of thin cigarette paper.

Cautiously smoothing the folded roll, and trying not to show her emotions, she began to read out the poetical dialogue ascribed to two famous Jewish Russian authors, Margarita Aliger and Ilya Ehrenburg, that was widely circulating among Jews in the "Samizdat," already in existence at that time. In this exchange, the writers expressed their bitterness and frustration at the persecution and violations of the civil rights of Jewish citizens in the postwar years.

What she read made my righteous indignation even deeper.

"Calm down, Vova. You can't escape what disturbs and revolts us," Zoya said, observing my reaction. "Just listen once again to what Margarita Aliger is saying in the letter she wrote soon after the war:

Warming hands in a house burned to ashes
I allowed a question to myself:
After all, who are we?
We are—*evrei* [the Jews]

How did I dare forget about that!
(translation by V. & M. Tsesis)

"The ways our people are treated in the country where we were born are mean, unfair, and cruel," Zoya continued. "And, remember, this is not the fault of the majority, but rather a problem with a small part of the population. But we must never give up. We must do what Jews have always done: survive in the name of the spark of life which was given to us when we were born. This is our responsibility to the thousands of years of our existence."

Zoya's words forever left a deep mark in my memory.

In the Soviet Union, anti-Semitism manifested itself in different degrees at different social levels. In the particular environment where I grew up, I had to face hatred and discrimination all the time.

Detestable individuals exist in every nation, and it was hard not to react to the omnipresent anti-Semitism, which ascribed the qualities of single ugly individuals among the Jews to the whole nation of Jews, especially if that anti-Semitism was accompanied by undisguised wishes for pain and physical destruction to be brought upon an entire people.

However, the Jews are not easily dispirited. Instead of being discouraged by such unfair treatment and becoming absorbed into other nations, the Jews refused to commit social suicide. Thousands of years of history have proven the legendary, incomprehensible ability of the Jewish people to adapt to the most unfavorable living conditions and, ignoring humiliation from their ill-wishers, to follow their own path and build their own lives. Among many important weapons for successful survival in the most unfavorable circumstances, Jews always had a powerful secret weapon: their unsurpassed sense of humor, along with its most precious feature—an infinite ability to laugh at themselves.

Today, little known by most people, a war of words is waged against the Jews by an army of international anonymous and not-so-anonymous bigots on electronic media. Thanks to the freedom of speech unique to Western democracies, people can publish whatever they want on Internet web pages and portals. Anyone can open YouTube or Facebook to be shocked by the ocean of rhetoric of evil and violence, very frequently accompanied by calls for physical extermination of opponents. One of the favorite targets for the outpouring of the basest human emotions since ancient times have always been the Jews. Day in and day out, bloody, ruthless, and, in essence, cannibalistic comments are directed toward them.

However, the Jews will never give up. Even a cursory analysis of what is going in the electronic media is sufficient to reassure an observer that—following the ancient traditions of our people—the Jews are fighting back with determination. Although the Jews make up only .24 percent of the world population, a disproportionately large number of them rebuff those who threaten Jewish people and try to degrade their human dignity. This happens around the clock and across the board. The descendants of the ancient Maccabees and Masada will never allow their enemies to make them victims of another—national or international—catastrophe. Never again.

The overwhelming majority of Jews are born and die as Jews. For them to disrespect their origin and to forget their identity means to betray their own selves.

FORGED BY HATRED

AFTER SEIZING POWER IN 1917, the Soviet regime tried to replace faith in God with communist ideology by all available means. However, to achieve such a goal proved to be much more difficult than it first seemed to the proponents of the new system. This confirmed the well-known truth that totalitarian systems are never fully able to replace man's inborn, ineradicable aspiration toward satisfaction of their deep spiritual needs with a surrogate ideology. Doing everything in its power, and having suppressed the competition, the pervasive Marxist-Leninist propaganda was still unable to erase the collective memory of religion, history, and culture. Because of its strong heritage, Russian civilization steadfastly withstood the endless gibberish of the Communist party line. Even the most oppressive and effective totalitarian regime fails when it tries to remove books from state or private libraries, because great writers and thinkers and their critical thought and ideas of God can never be thoroughly censored.

Many works published in the Soviet Union, both by Russian authors and by foreign authors in translation, contained not only content satisfying the authorities but also views contradicting the official ideology. For example, books that discussed individual freedom met the official censors' demands and were included in school and university curricula. A careful reader of such writers as Pushkin, Gogol,

Dostoyevsky, Tolstoy, and Gorki could find plenty of sedition in their works and, after carefully analyzing them, would develop a keen and sharp critical mind.

Violating human respect and dignity, anti-Semitism in Soviet society was carefully directed by the patronizing hand of the Communist party. One could find frequent anti-Semitism in many books and in international and local news broadcasts on TV and radio, and satirical articles featuring characters with typical Jewish family names. If the family name was not enough to betray ethnic origin, the authors used the first names and patronymics of the characters. Even the most thick-skinned Jew facing such omnipresent propaganda could not help but take it as a personal insult.

My first encounter with anti-Semitism occurred when I was five, in 1946. It happened not long after my mother, my brother, and I returned from an evacuation in the city of Andijan in Uzbekistan. After joining my father in the territory of the Karelo-Finnish Autonomous Republic, where he had continued his military service after the war, we moved to a small military town at the Pontonnaya Station not far from Leningrad.

One day in August, my mother, humming some Ukrainian song, comfortably settled herself in the middle of our yard, cut a big bar of soap into pieces, put them into a large tub, poured hot water from a pail into the tub, and started doing laundry.

Dressed in short pants with narrow fabric suspenders and in a splendid mood, I hung around next to her, trying to help her when she asked for it. Suddenly peace and quiet were disturbed by a thin, teasing voice.

About thirty yards away from us, a girl around ten years old stood on the pavement and, pointing her small finger at me and then at my mother, sang loudly: "Zhid, Zhid, Zhid, hangs on the little rope. . ." By the cocky tone in which she sang, I could understand that it was supposed to be an insult to us. Having repeated the song from the popular anti-Semitic "folk art" repertoire several times, the girl stuck out her tongue, turned around and ran down the street.

Before that, I had never heard the word "Zhid."

"Mummy, what does the word "Zhid" mean?" I asked my mother who, looking sad and pale, mopped flocks of soapy foam from her hands.

"That is a very ugly word," she answered, as she stroked my head and looked away. "Do not repeat it, Vova, and please do not pay attention to those who will say that word to you in the future."

"Why? Why is that word ugly?"

"Because. . . When the time comes, you, unfortunately, will know about it well yourself," my mother answered in a soft, muffled voice. She angrily waved her fist in the direction the offender had disappeared to and then went back to her laundry.

In the same year, the military unit my father served in moved to Viborg, a city also in the Leningrad District.

One sunny day, my fourteen-year-old brother took me to the center of the city. Tired after the long walk, we sat on the lower steps of the big, wooden platform standing in the middle of the central square paved with cobbles. Not far from us, two beautiful young women met each other and started to talk. They were dressed in stylish summer outfits and high heels, which were quite rare in the post-war period.

Their lively conversation was suddenly interrupted when one of the women stopped talking and, with her face contortted from the effort, looked intently at us in amazement. At last, having reached the desirable conclusion, she said to her friend, loudly and indignantly, so that everyone around us could hear her:

"Look at them, Zinaida! So young and already Jewish. I wonder where these big-nosed boys have come from!"

"You are right, indeed," the other woman reacted, even more loudly, looking in our direction, "Hitler was, of course, a big bastard creating so much evil, but about one thing he was right: he gave hell to that population."

Seeing how pale my brother's face became, I realized that the woman had said something very offensive. My brother did not want to discuss with me what had happened and only later did I understand what these horrible words meant.

After many similar episodes—sometimes they occurred every day in my young years—I could not have any doubts as to what people I belonged to. If I ever forgot it for even a moment, someone with an unhealthy enthusiasm would definitely remind me who I was.

* * *

The word "Jew" implies belonging to a particular ethnic and cultural group as well as to the religion of Judaism. Therefore, from an early age, anti-Semitism appeared to me in different guises.

My school years passed in the town of Beltsy, situated in the north of what was then the Moldavian Socialist Republic. The only synagogue in this town with a sizable Jewish population was housed rather far from the center of the town in a small, primitive building on Kishinevskaya Street. I saw this building only from the outside and would learn what was going on there mostly from my father, who, despite his outwardly negative attitude to religion, and ignoring my presence in the room, never missed an opportunity to discuss with my mother in Yiddish urban news and rumors concerning different Jewish interests.

It was in the early 1960s when my father told us about the fire in the synagogue, resulting in most of the synagogue being burned down. Judging from the material evidence, it was arson. An investigation performed by the militia predictably did not find the culprits.

One month after the fire, the local religious Jews managed to collect a small amount of money, enough to restore the building.

Having successfully overcome preliminary bureaucratic difficulties, all that was left for the Jewish community to obtain permission to renovate the synagogue was merely nothing. This "mere nothing" was an approval for the work issued by the local KGB, or more precisely by the "Committee for Jewish Affairs" of the KGB, which took a "paternal" interest in the life of the local Jewish community. No other nationalities in the Soviet Union were given such an "honor."

"What do you want?" asked the head of the local KGB, Ippolit Popov, when the venerable elders gathered in his office to get permission for repairs. Then, without waiting for their answer, he continued, "Your building doesn't require any special repairs! One of the rooms of the synagogue was left practically undamaged, and you should be thankful, since—just so you know—it could have been much worse. You can pray in that room, old men. There is quite enough space there.

I guess that does it, and do not disturb me anymore! I am a busy man!"

"But, Comrade Popov, we are not asking for state funding. We are able to restore the synagogue with the money we have raised from believers," protested the visitors.

"And I am saying to you that you are not permitted to use your private initiative, comrade Jews. Please, do not try my patience with all your questions!" Popov harshly retorted.

"Comrade Popov, the room you are talking about is just a very small utility room. It is absolutely impossible to pray there, since our religious service requires the presence of at least ten people. Once again we are asking you to kindly give us permission for reconstruction at the expense of our own Jewish community. We commit ourselves not to cause anyone any inconvenience."

"What do you want me to do, comrade Jews?! Do you think I am my own boss? I am not authorized to make any decisions without consent from above. Forget it. And you," Popov said, pointing a finger at one of the visitors, "you'd better tell me what your surname is. Aha, Friedman! Now tell me, Friedman, does your son work for a design institution here in Beltsy? Does he? Okay. Great. Is he happy at his job? You say he is. So listen, father, to what I am going to tell you. You surely want your son to keep his good job at the design office, right? So tell me, don't you think you have to give up your Zionist activities for the sake of your only son? Tell me!"

"But it has nothing to do with what you call 'Zionist activities,' Comrade Popov. The only thing we want is to restore our synagogue," Friedman dared to object.

"We are done! I don't want to hear any more about your synagogue, Jews. And please, do not provoke me anymore. We don't touch you, so you, too, leave us alone. Is it clear?"

It took two years of navigating government regulations and prohibitions before the courageous—they could be called so—elderly Jews were able to obtain permission for restoration of the synagogue. This happened mostly because of an unforeseen development: members of an American delegation coming to Beltsy expressed their wish to visit the local Jewish place of worship.

GOD IN THE PIONEER CAMP

IN THE SUMMER OF 1949, when I was eight years old, my parents decided to present me with a gift. They thought that during my first summer vacation I would be excited to spend a month in a pioneer camp, where, my parents assured me, I would be very happy. Like any child in a similar situation, I could not wait to get to that unknown place where I would be in a new environment and meet new children.

The pioneer camp was located a few hours away, in Kishinev (now Chisinau), the capital of Moldova. Early in the morning, my father and I boarded an intercity bus. We arrived in the center of Kishinev at noon. It took us quite a long time to find the pioneer camp, which was located far away on the outskirts of the city. My first—and last—stay at the pioneer camp began when, hastily saying goodbye and giving me a brief kiss, my father left, leaving me in the care of counselors. It did not take long for me to discover how hard it is to live without those who love you. What a difficult time it was for me!

At the pioneer camp, I became a boy whose name nobody remembered, whose face hardly anyone could memorize. Though at the camp I was given food and something to drink and put to bed on time, as a person I was abandoned, without personal care or company.

There was no way to call home by phone, and even if that had been possible, I was too young to be able to express to my parents all the intensity of my despair. I learned then that it is better to live with those you love in the poorest place than to be an orphan in a royal palace.

However, every cloud has a silver lining. One day near the end of my stay at the camp, for the first and last time during that miserable month, a cinema operator visited the camp to show us pioneers a movie. In anticipation of that extraordinary event, the whole pioneer camp was buzzing like a beehive and, without doubt, our high hopes—at least mine—came true beyond all expectations. Oh, what a wonderful film the movie projectionist showed us! It was the best movie I've ever seen in my life!

In the community hall a white bed sheet was stretched over the wall, serving as a movie screen. A motion-picture projection machine was placed on a tripod. His every move followed by the impatient curious glances of the children starving for any kind of entertainment, the movie projectionist, accompanied by the characteristic metallic sound, took the first spool out of one of two big tin canisters. The machine started to rattle and the miracle began. And really, what a miracle it was! I temporarily became an abandoned thing, who, it turned out, had not forgotten how to laugh loudly and how to have fun and enjoy life. Lucky me: never before did I have an opportunity to see the cinematic masterpiece *Vesyolie Rebyata—The Jolly Fellows*. That film took me back to the world of joy and humor from which I was temporarily barred. My return to that normal world served as the prelude to what happened the next day.

That day on the playground, where I used to spend time with other children, I had the first and the last chance to meet and speak to a Moldavian boy called Georgiy, who was probably a year older than me. Georgiy lived with his parents not far from the camp and had come alone that day to hang around with the children on the camp playground, located in the church garden. The church itself was of a beautiful, original architecture. Its massive door faced the road along which rural huts stood at a distance from one another.

A friendly boy, Georgiy was thin, tall, and of rather dark complexion. He was dressed in a loose black shirt with big white buttons. We got so carried away with our conversation that we did not notice that it had gradually become dark. Soon the children playing in the garden went back to the camp, and we remained there all alone. As we discussed different things, Georgiy and I slowly approached the garden gate, walking along the path lined with old trees.

In the gathering dusk, Georgiy mentioned once again word I had never heard before: God. I asked him what it meant.

"God is the One who is in heaven," answered Georgiy confidently. "My dad and my mom, they know everything. They told me that God sees all, knows all, and helps all the people, but especially us children."

The last thing he said pleased me most of all.

"There is no one greater than God," my first religious enlightener continued with conviction.

"He can do anything. God is in heaven, in the air, among the trees, everywhere, in every place. He is always with us," my young mentor stated with certainty.

"But where is He? Can we see Him? Where is He! Does He see us now?" I asked Georgiy impatiently.

"If you watch carefully, you may be lucky and see Him. God is in heaven, in the sea, in the air. . . Everywhere. Everywhere. Everywhere. He is watching us and comes to our help, when we need Him."

"But how can God watch everyone at the same time? Where is He? Does He see us now? Could He be over there now, at the trees?!"

"Yes, and there, too. We just have to look very carefully to be able to recognize Him."

Little by little the gathering dusk began to intensify the bright light of the rising moon sailing up from the horizon. The moonbeams made their way through the tree crowns, spreading a wide, openwork lace of shadows on the paths and grass in the garden.

The definition of God that I heard from that boy, whom I never saw again, as simple and childish as it was, produced a lasting impression on me. In that memorable episode, I, a painfully lonely child, temporarily abandoned and cut off from my familiar life, passionately yearned to see He who would never forget about me and who would not be indifferent to my presence.

With my eyes wide open, I stared into the darkness, trying to discern the face of my Guardian, who seemed to care for me, a tiny breathing dot in the vast expanse of the universe.

I was so anxious for my wish to come true that, to my amazement, a vision suddenly appeared before my young eyes: it seemed to me that, first on the top of the thick trunk of one tree, and then on another, in the vague outlines I saw His face, the face of Him who will never leave me and who will never abandon me. Having reached the gates of the church's garden, Georgiy and I parted. He went home, and I headed for the pioneer camp. I never had another chance to meet that mystical stranger, the boy named Georgiy, who told me for the first time in my life that the One, whom I subconsciously sought, indeed existed.

In every human being, there is a desire to meet Him who gives meaning to his or her life. One part of humanity is trying to suppress that desire by all sorts of distractions, while the other part, greater in number, cannot imagine life without faith in His Divine Presence.

IN GOD'S HAND

I DO NOT BELIEVE in dreams and superstitions for the simple reason that the tangible reality we encounter in everyday life presents itself to us with a cornucopia of mysteries. We need only examine what initially appears common and mundane to discover another previously unnoticed small miracle.

But about half a century after my encounter with Georgiy, I had an unforgettable dream in which I had an intuitive awareness of Divine Presence. The dream I had was very special. Dreams are rarely accompanied by emotions. For example, when we see in our dreams wild beasts ready to attack us or people ready to kill us, or when we expect to fall into a gorge, instead of the fear and panic we might feel if we were awake, we most frequently perceive these events tranquilly as if we were witnesses rather than live participants. However, sometimes we have an opportunity to have dreams which, though nothing extraordinary happens, we perceive as something prophetic, resisting rational explanation.

In one such memorable, rare dream I observed myself from afar: another me sat on a sled riding down a steep snowy hill. The sled gradually gathered momentum, and, in a short time, I was rushing down the hill at a breakneck speed. Suddenly, I realized that soon I would lose control. I tried unsuccessfully to slow the sled down by using my feet, but instead the speed increased until I felt that I could do nothing to stop it.

Another second and the sled would fly into dangerously sharp branches sticking out of shrubs on both sides of the hill.

I had no emotions during this dream. I felt that it was all happening not to the real me, but to my clone. My mind perceived the events as something trivial and indifferent, even when the sled soared high up into the sky. All of a sudden my clone disappeared, and the real me was on that sled as it flew up into the sky. If the sled were to fall, my life would inevitably be taken away. At that moment, when the disaster seemed unavoidable, something totally unexpected happened: a big, caring, invisible hand picked up my sled as if it were a light little feather and immediately took control of my flight.

I will forever remember that feeling of a huge hand cautiously and confidently carrying me on its protective Palm to complete safety. Before waking up I was overwhelmed with high emotions, a mental state that happens after very important encounters in our life.

"It was just a dream, nothing more! Stop believing illusions," one part of my consciousness said to me, but the other part of it hammered my mind with a thought: "It was Him! It was Him!"

In the following days, I gradually forgot this unusual dream and probably would not attach a special meaning to it if it had not been for another real life episode that occurred a week later.

On that day I was driving on the highway, heading to my office for the morning ambulatory hours. The traffic was great, visibility was excellent, and the day was sunny and clear. Before getting into the exit lane on my right toward the ramp, in the side mirror I clearly saw the reflection of a big, dark red truck, moving at a normal speed.

Making sure, or so it seemed to me, that the truck was at a safe distance, I pushed on the gas pedal in order to enter the exit lane. The maneuver had been practically accomplished when I heard the loud, unmistakable sound of a crash, a shattering blow to the back of my car. I instantly recalled that huge vehicle driving behind me and realized that it had hit me.

After a crash like that, my car would have turned over, hit the traffic barrier, and then bounced back. My hands impulsively clutched the steering wheel even though it was totally useless in such an accident. In a situation like that, there is no time for fear or for a prayer; resigned and emotionless in anticipation of inevitable tragedy, I waited for what would happen next.

However, what seemed inevitable did not happen. Instead of turning over, my car, as if it were led by an invisible large hand, continued moving forward on the right lane of the expressway in a surprisingly steady and confident manner. Moreover, it was gradually and comfortably slowing down. Could things settle down in this incredible way? How could that happen?

And in that fraction of a second, realizing that, by a miracle, I had narrowly escaped a disastrous end, my memory revived the recent dream. I remembered the mighty hand that on both occasions had helped me to escape my imminent demise.

However, this time it was not my sled rushing to disaster. It happened in reality: the invisible mighty hand had really saved my life.

I could not understand how I had remained safe and unharmed after the violent crash.

I opened the door of my car and stepped out onto the shoulder of the expressway, looking around. To my surprise,

I noticed that as a result of the crash the rear bumper of my car had slipped under the front bumper of the huge truck that had just hit me. So this is how I escaped inevitable death! Interlocked with bumpers our vehicles became one whole. No efforts on my part to control the car after the shattering crash would have been successful if my bumper had not, in an inconceivable manner, perfectly matched the bumper of the truck, forming an inseparable pair with it.

One can see my time had not yet come!

The window of the truck was open, and I heard. . . laughter. I looked up. In the cabin of the truck, the driver and the passenger were talking and laughing, pointing their fingers at me. Why are they laughing, I wondered, when their truck almost killed me a minute ago?

The driver of the truck, as if reading my mind, explained:

"Listen, man, until I realized you became a part of my car, I bet my friend twenty dollars that you wouldn't survive the accident, and now, because you were so lucky, I've lost my bet. But don't you worry," he concluded, smiling widely, "even though you've let me down, I'm not mad at you."

The driver and his friend resumed their laughter. For me, there was nothing else left to do but to join their fun.

Almost immediately, traffic police officers arrived; for them another car accident did not present anything special. After a cursory evaluation of the episode, they stated that whatever happened was a mutual fault. Neither the truck driver nor I was ticketed.

American efficiency: not even five minutes passed before a tow truck appeared. On the roads of America, all problems are resolved quickly. Skillfully lifting the back of my car with a large winch, the driver effortlessly managed to detach the rear bumper of my car from the tight iron embrace of the big truck's front bumper, and then, as if nothing special had happened I turned the ignition, started my car, and soon was in my office, arriving only a little late for the morning reception of patients.

Was my miraculous escape from certain death just a chance happening or the result of involvement of the invisible hand, which I had felt so vividly in my dream a week before? Was this powerful hand mysteriously saving me from another impending disaster? At many times in my life when troubles occurred, at the last moment something unexpected would happen, which would safely resolve the critical situation I had just faced.

If I were an atheist, after that accident I would have thought I was just lucky, but being a believer, I could not help but think that I was obliged to the grace of heaven for my survival.

And who knows? Who knows? Maybe the High Authority took into account that that morning I had participated in the worship services. Only God knows whether I am right or wrong about that.

BETWEEN LIFE AND DEATH

RELIGION HAS ALWAYS BEEN an integral part of human history, and it will always be integral for the individual from birth, throughout life and the withdrawal from life, to the inevitable, death. Indeed, the fact that human life is limited in both time and space has forever been one of the major reasons why people turn to religion where they can find satisfying answers to otherwise incomprehensible questions: why we are born, why we die.

"Death is the midwife of philosophy," the famous phrase says. Non-believers, rejecting the concept of the eternal soul, seek answers to the fundamental question of existence in the boundless field of philosophy. However, any time a philosophical system states that it has such an explanation, another philosophical system soon denies that claim as incorrect.

In this respect nothing can replace religion. Real religion—not its countless fanatic and nonsensical caricatures, where religion is used for different sinister purposes—is not a fancy, or wishful thinking, or the product of a sick imagination, or, as Karl Marx said, "opium of the people."

Many people try to avoid thoughts about death at any cost, day after day putting off this inevitability to the indefinite future. To this phenomenon of the human psyche, the late Ernest Becker dedicated his classic book *The Denial of Death*.

Still others, instead of hiding their heads in the sand like ostriches, yearn to know why the splendid dance of life eventually gives place to eternal peace, why the dazzling sunlight of our planet changes into the thick darkness of nonexistence.

Death is an integral part of life, urging human beings to seek the reason for their existence on Earth. When people finally and truly understand that representatives of the human race are but short-term guests in this world, there is nothing that can replace in them the meaning of God, the God who embedded inside of us an eternal undying spirit. If we sincerely wish to come closer to the truth about who we are on this tiny Earth, soaked with sweat and blood, surrounded by the unbounded spaces of the unending universe, sooner or later, all roads lead to the search for the Creator.

My first encounter with death occurred when I was six and attended kindergarten. Not far from the school was a little hill in the city park, and our teachers took us to sled there during the winter.

One snowy day our group went up toward the hill, each of us holding the hand of another child. My partner was Tanya, a girl who always sat next to me at dinnertime. She was a cheerful girl who amused everybody around her. Our relationship was special, because she did not like Russian-style fruit compote and would always share it with me. After experiencing hunger during the war, I was left for the rest of my life with a healthy appetite.

Tanya and I laughed and talked so loudly on the way to the hill that our teacher asked us to be quiet several times. There were a lot of kids there when we arrived; their shouts and loud laughter resonated in the air. The children sledded down in the relatively narrow passage between chain-link fences attached to metal poles.

Tanya and I shared a ride. I sat in the front, and she was behind me. During the ride, our sled was pushed from both sides by other kids. Every time we wanted to slip away from the next push or pull, we were hit again by sleds from the opposite side. After one especially strong strike, we sped toward the metal post of the fence. I managed to roll off the sled, but Tanya, tightly clutching the edges, remained sitting until the sled reached the fence at high speed and loudly crashed against it.

Tanya was flung off the sled; her forehead smashed straight against the metal pole. Hitting her head hard, she let out a desperate shrill scream. By the time the children ran to see what happened, the teacher was already there. She threw herself on Tanya's body, tightly embracing her and, screaming loudly, desperately begged the girl to answer her. Tanya did not respond, with each moment becoming more pale and lifeless. She, who was so happy only seconds before, with her eyes sparkling and a snow white smile, was now motionless, her head thrown back and deprived of life. Something invisible left her face, which had been so excited a very short time ago. That "something" was replaced by what later I, as a physician in similar situations, called "the mask of death."

The teacher, with Tanya in her arms, surrounded by the group of adults and children, ran down to the road at the bottom of the hill.

The next day, we were told that Tanya died from a skull fracture. That was the first time I witnessed the death, so close and so dramatic, of a human being—a child.

It was difficult for me to recover after the indescribable transformation I had seen. Since then, I have never ceased to be moved by the impossible-to-describe moment when a careful observer—perhaps by a sixth sense—can detect that fleeting instant when the non-material soul leaves forever what had just been a warm, breathing body.

Four years later, I experienced another episode, which even more clearly and more tangibly taught me that human life is nothing more than a fragile, temporary experience.

Our house and our family's small vegetable garden next to it faced a cobbled town road. The other side of the garden was bordered by a walkway covered with crushed stone mixed with dirt and leading to the houses in the middle of our block. The vegetable garden, of modest size, was one of the places where I enjoyed spending time "talking" to cucumbers, tomatoes, radishes, and even the weeds.

One August afternoon, humming some song while examining young sprouts of vegetables, I realized that someone was watching me. Raising my eyes, I saw an elderly woman standing on the walkway. Her adoring gaze was directed toward me.

Though I did not know the name of this woman, I knew she was Jewish and that she lived somewhere nearby. I remembered well her haggard face covered with a web of deep wrinkles. I had seen her many times before when she passed by our house dressed in plain cheap clothes, always in a hurry, carrying a worn black bag. I never thought that this woman paid any attention to me or even suspected my existence.

One of the pleasant aspects of childhood—and I am sure many of us miss this when we grow up—is adults loudly expressing their delight and admiration at the sight of us, the fascinating, growing creatures. Looking at me, the old woman was probably moved by my carefree childish appearance, which, no doubt, reminded her of her own forever-departed childhood. Literally caressing me with her eyes—what a precious gaze it was—the woman gave me an admiring and radiant smile with her gap-toothed mouth. In that postwar period, many old people lacked teeth.

"A *tayer ingl* ('precious boy')," she addressed me in Yiddish. "What a *nevroku*, a *shein kind* ('what a nice child') your mother and father have!" "*Zol di zain gezint!* ('may you be healthy!')," she said at parting, admiring to her heart's content what she had seen in me, and, vigorously waving goodbye, briskly went about her business.

Like any other child, I took compliments like these for granted and continued to play in the garden.

Later in the day, following my mother's strict order, I practiced scales and arpeggios on the violin in our garden gazebo. Suddenly, I heard loud female cries coming from the middle of the street. The crying continued for quite a while, and I went to see what was happening. I put aside the violin and, following the sound, soon reached the place from which the crying came.

I saw a typical poor Bessarabian hut in front of which gathered a small group of people. Some of the women loudly sobbed, wiping away tears—for the time and place, a typical display of unconcealed grief when someone died—while the men were quiet.

Through the open hut door, I noticed that the corridor was crowded with people. Unimpeded by anyone, I entered the house. Along the walls and in the middle of the room on plain chairs sat people I did not know with solemn, sad expressions on their faces. In front of them, on a rough homespun rug thrown on a clay-painted dirt floor, lay a dead old woman. Looking closely at her, to my surprise, I at once recognized the old Jewish woman who such a short time before had been alive and giving me admiring looks. That woman, whose invisible thread of life and destiny intersected with the path of my own fate just minutes before, no longer existed as a person.

A shocking truth was revealed to me again in stark nakedness: death, which hides cunningly behind life, can exercise its power whenever it wants; life is a non-negotiated wonderful gift that can be taken away at any time.

Everyone Dies Alone is the title of a book by German writer Hans Fallada, which quite impressed me when I read it in my childhood. By the time I saw the old woman dead on the carpet, I had already realized that there was no point in asking adults why human life had a beginning and an end. It took many years until I understood that I could not expect to receive an unequivocal answer; each individual comes to this answer according to his or her unique world view.

* * *

Another encounter with death happened one late afternoon on my way home as I passed by the corner of Dostoyevsky and Staropochtovaya streets in Beltsy. A small group of people were waiting for a bus. I was about to cross the street when directly in front of me a slightly plump, medium-height woman dressed in overalls suddenly uttered a heartrending, shrill cry and slowly fell to her knees. Her face was contorted with pain. She gasped for breath, and from her throat escaped hoarse, chilling, dreary moans. While she tried her best to resist the progressing weakness, fresh pieces of raw meat wrapped in coarse grey paper started to fall out of her pockets and from some other secret places of her working clothes. Finally her legs gave way, and she fell on her back, for a short time clinging to life, which was quickly leaving her. She was motionless, piteously groaning, and then she was silent.

Several people rushed to help the woman. One of them, a middle-aged man, performed a primitive CPR: he blew in her face and tried to find her pulse. Later he and another man started moving her hands up and down—Silvester's method of resuscitation, in use at that time in Russia. Soon the first man raised his head and said:

"That's all. The woman is dead. Call the militia and the ambulance. Tell them a woman's body needs to be taken to the morgue."

Everybody around was bewildered by the sudden death of the woman who minutes before had seemed healthy and strong. One of the adults standing next to me said that the woman passed away because of a heart attack or a stroke.

"Such an unfortunate woman. For sure, she worked at the slaughterhouse," he continued confidently, pointing to the packets of meat still lying scattered on the ground. "Look at the meat. She stole it from there and probably was afraid to be caught red-handed any minute."

I still associate the sight of raw meat with the woman in overalls lying lifeless on the pavement.

* * *

Another memorable dramatic scene of the passing of life, which reminded me once again of the tragic ordinariness of death, happened when I was in eighth grade. In the evening twilight I was walking beside the iron fence of Beltsy's so-called Children's Park, when the silence of the peaceful environment was broken by the shrill sound of a militiaman's whistle, and shortly after that, the loud sounds of two gunshots. After another short pause, I heard the whistle again. Not thinking much about the possible consequences, and intrigued to know what was happening, I found a gap in the fence and walked in the direction of the shots I had just heard. Somewhere close to me, perhaps a hundred feet away, I heard indistinct voices. Making my way through the darkness and stumbling over branches and bumps, I eventually reached the site of the incident.

In the middle of a small clearing I saw a few onlookers. Opposite the group stood a middle-aged man, neatly dressed in a sports jacket, carefully ironed pants, and a tie. In his straightened arm, hanging toward the ground, he held a medium-sized pistol. Such pistols were usually carried by state officials in a buttoned holster. Obviously, the man was an undercover militia officer. In front of him, face-down on the ground, lay the motionless body of a young man. Without a doubt, it was the man who had just been shot. Everybody in the group was silent until someone dared to speak.

"You seem to be from the militia, comrade," he politely addressed the man with the gun.

"What else? Of course I am. Keeping order in the area like I am supposed to."

"And what happened here, why did you have to shoot this man? Is he a criminal?"

The militiaman could have kept silent, but it seemed as if the recent killing of an unarmed man was affecting his conscience. He needed to vent his feelings.

"He has only himself to blame! I was patrolling the park and saw him at a distance holding a bag in his hands," the militia officer said, pointing with the tip of his shoe in the direction of the dead man lying on the ground. "Recently in this district there have been several thefts and robberies. That's why I was patrolling here. I suspected he was carrying something he had just stolen and I ordered him to stop, but this fool, instead of obeying my order, tried to run away. Three times I shouted at him as loudly as I could, twice I blew my militia whistle, but instead of stopping, as law-abiding citizens are required to do, this idiot ran even faster than before. There was nothing else for me to do but to shoot at him. What could I have done? Those are the regulations."

"Oh, I understand. So that's what it is. You were performing your duties," the onlooker uttered respectfully. "I did not know that parks were also patrolled."

"Sure enough. We are all over. That's what militia is all about. That's why we are militia."

"So, what was this guy carrying in his bag?"

"What, what? Here it is, you can see for yourself." The plainclothes militiaman, visibly annoyed, pointed at the coarse knitted bag lying not far from us. "Glass containers. Empty bottles, jars. Nothing else. Wanted to get some money for them. I can't understand why this stupid guy did not stop. Do you really think I wanted to shoot him?"

"Of course not. Of course not, officer. You were just performing your duty. It's understandable," the man hastened to reply.

"Anyway, what is done is done," said the militia officer, this time carelessly poking with the tip of his shoe at the body of the innocent victim he had just killed. "Nothing can be changed anyway. My shift ended an hour ago, but now, because of him, I have to contact the militia and have him taken to the morgue. Let me whistle once again for help."

This incident was like a scene from a madhouse. The law enforcer did not even try to hide the fact that he had shot and killed an unarmed man, whose only fault was that he did not stop, while the public reacted as if that was the way it should be.

Growing up, I found out that the surrealistic scene I had witnessed was quite common in the country where Stalin's methods of maintaining civil order by "using a firm hand" were considered the unshakable norm for dealing with people. At that time, protected by the rules of the totalitarian state, representatives of law and order could arbitrarily violate human rights. In that sort of society, human life—as far as those in power are concerned—loses its sanctity and is treated as a commodity. Laws of humanity begin only when each human life is treated as a sacred, unique, and irreplaceable gift from heaven.

* * *

When I was nine years old I witnessed a display of immense cruelty, not toward a human being, but toward a harmless lap dog. Unlike in today's Western urban environment, the children of my age in Russia used to spend plenty of time outdoors on the streets or in the neighborhood backyards. Not far from us were houses where the families of military personnel lived. In the middle of the block was a primitive playground. Children from the neighborhood liked to spend time there. Among other features the playground included a sand pit for the little children.

One pleasant, warm afternoon, we were playing hide-and-seek. I was running, trying to find the hidden players, when we heard the desperate yelp of a dog. Interrupting our game, we rushed in the direction of the disturbing sound.

We saw a man dressed in the military uniform of a captain pulling a snow-white, adorable lap dog on a leash. In his free hand, the man held a standard officer's gun. On his face was the determined and threatening expression of an executioner. The officer pulled the dog toward the sand pit where kids were playing with sand pie molds, while the dog resisted as hard as it could, digging its little legs into the ground.

Perplexed, everyone who was in the yard at that time—boys and girls and some adults—gathered in a tight circle around the sand pit, to the center of which the man pulled the struggling dog. The dog's wild yelp drowned the voices of the people gathered around.

"What has this dog done to you? Why are you dragging it here?" one of the adults asked the captain loudly.

"Will tell you later," he answered and, pointing the muzzle of the pistol at the desperately struggling lap dog on the leash, cocked the gun. Taking aim and firing three shots, he killed at close range the little white dog who did not want to die. The lap dog let out a desperate howl and fell on the sand, staining with dog's blood the place where moments before kids peacefully played with sand pie molds.

"So why did you finish off this dog? You still did not tell us anything," the man again asked the officer, while the lap dog writhed in deadly convulsions, gradually succumbing to eternal sleep.

"Oh, yes, excuse me. I totally forgot I've promised to explain to you," the officer answered, with the air of a person satisfied that he had just performed a duty toward the whole of society.

A minute before he was acting like a madman, and now, like a melodramatic actor on the stage, he effortlessly regained the appearance of a civilized person.

"You see, my three-year-old daughter was playing with the dog and pulled her tail. You know—a child. So the dog caught her finger and bit her so hard that she bled. But it's okay now. No biting anymore by that dog."

What could be said? The people stood silent, shocked by what they had just witnessed. Probably in the Stone Age, many thousands of years ago, people were less cruel than are modern pseudo-educated savages, whom society entrusts with power and weapons.

"DEATH, BE NOT PROUD"

YOUTH HYPNOTIZES US. Observing the pace, movement, grace, excited smiles, and burning glances of young people, one would think that they will always stay youthful and healthy. But in reality human life is transient and fragile. Among many other important reasons prompting me to turn to religion as a source of truth, I always had a desire to reconcile myself to the finiteness of human life, so strongly contrasting with the eternity of the universe. My profession has been an important factor in the development of my views on this aspect of existence.

Right after graduating from medical school, I started to work as a rural district pediatrician in a relatively large Moldavian village called Malaieshti. My hospital, situated about ten miles from the town of Tiraspol, was a collecting point for all the serious illnesses that affected the children in the district villages. I experienced tremendous emotional stress working there mostly because of the frequent deaths of children, especially babies. Intestinal infections were the main cause of death. Usually, the children were brought from the neighboring villages in such a degree of dehydration that it was already impossible to help them with the level of medical care available at that time. It is a real nightmare for a physician to lose children's lives, especially when you are absolutely powerless, when all that is left is to see how they are dying.

Later, working as a doctor at Odessa Infectious Diseases Hospital, I had another dreadfully emotionally draining experience involving death—this time, the deaths of many adult patients.

I was an active part of a medical team providing critical care to the people who had the misfortune to contract illness during the outbreak of cholera in Odessa in 1970. This epidemic took the lives of sixteen adults—a level of mortality far exceeding world standards.

Aside from the truly traumatic and tragic experiences I had as a physician losing the lives of many children and adults, I learned a lesson not described in any medical textbook: every time I witnessed the moment of death of a patient of any age, I had the same indescribable, mystical feeling that a curtain was falling in the play called "Life." What was only a moment before a pulsating, tangible, living body was replaced by life-lessness, stiffness, an eternal silence of the inanimate body devoid of the brilliant light of the human spirit.

People who see the bare truth of the phenomenon of human existence cannot fail to be impressed by the sheer power of death. Limitation of human life in time and space is one of the major starting points urging us to search for an explanation of human existence and eventually to choose the path of religion.

Many people prefer to deny death, consciously or subconsciously closing their eyes to what is the real truth. It's understandable: for them it might be too frightening to think about what is inevitable and beyond their control. Mankind has resorted to countless ways of self-deception and diversions to forget that a human life span is limited, that sooner or later death will knock with its bony finger on every closed door.

However, people who are not afraid to think about the taboo topic of death will always exist; they do not try to avoid such questions as what is the meaning of life, what do people live for, why do they die.

It may sound paradoxical, but, for people who believe in God, the idea of life's temporal limitation is not as pessimistic as might be expected! Indeed, the content of human life acquires unlimited optimism if God's presence and belief in the immortality of the human spirit are taken into account. If God was so generous that amid the immense ocean of the universe He granted us the absolutely inconceivable miracles of life and consciousness, if God granted people joy and pleasure in life on this planet, then this merciful God will not allow the precious content of earthly life to turn into the Theater of the Absurd, where, according to Shakespeare, "All the world's a stage, and all the men and women merely players," but will grant—incomprehensible as it is to the human mind—the possibility that our immortal spirits will live forever.

It might be noted that such attitude is typical of Judaism, because, unlike other monotheistic religions, Judaism has never focused on threatening people with brimstone, fear, and horror surrounding death.

Atheists like to say that people do not die completely; they continue to live perpetually thanks to the legacy they leave. All their good deeds live forever in their children and in the whole of humanity. The naïve simplicity of such understanding of what human life is all about is illustrated in a story by the popular late writer and journalist Malcolm Muggeridge. One of his memoirs detail the years he spent in India, where as a young man he taught English to local children and spent his leisure time conversing with interesting people. In the community where he lived there was an elderly guru held in high respect by the locals. Muggeridge took great interest in the opinions of this wise man. Once, being deeply impressed with the guru's intellect, the future writer suggested that the wise man write a book about his own philosophy in order to help those who would be interested in his fresh and original ideas. The guru smiled in response—apparently he had already considered such a proposal.

"Well, tell me how long a book lives?" he asked Malcolm Muggeridge. Then he added, "Inanimate things disappear in the waters of Lethe just as fast as people, so is it worth wasting my life's precious, irretrievable time to write something that lasts only temporarily?"

The words of the Indian wise man echoed with what is written in one of the books of the Jewish Bible, Ecclesiastes (12:12): ". . . Of making many books there is no end, and much study wearies the body. . ."

Human history is like a theatrical stage, on the scaffold of which new generations constantly take the place of previous ones. What was urgent and vital yesterday is forgotten forever and replaced by what is urgent and vital today. For the Jews of many generations, the Torah has been the ever-living, immortal word of God to His people, which unites all generations by common ethics, common attitude to objective reality, and by common acknowledgement of the importance of human life and our mission on earth.

Compared to the age of the universe, human life, even if it lasted for three hundred years, would only be a glimpse. Therefore a long and hopefully happy life is not the answer to the mystery of human existence. Only through faith in God can human beings unite with eternity. The negative aspects of life that accompany individuals—problems with health, aging, emotional pain—are much easier to overcome and live with when there is faith in God. Belief in God makes the life of each human being highly significant, turning every fleeting moment of existence into a precious gift.

Our individual selves, which today are pulsating and vigorous, inescapably and mercilessly approach disappearance from the face of this planet. But our fleeting existence could be perceived not as a tragedy but as a powerful stimulus to participate in God's cosmic plan and to perfect our souls in anticipation of eternal life. God loves us and God is worthy of our love and gratitude, not least for creating each of us from the stardust of the universe, for endowing us with inquisitive minds, creative consciousness, and an infinite sense of humor, and for giving us His Torah—a guide to life connecting mortality with eternity.

In the vast ocean of the universe, only we—representatives of the human race living on a planet that appears as a small dot within the Milky Way galaxy—are able to see, hear, and feel God's world and perceive cosmic order in God's creation.

No matter what tomorrow has in store for us, no one can ever take away the great meaning of what we have lived through, the precious memories of those who loved us and whom we loved. The concept of death, perceived as nothing other than a moment that separates our earthly life from the life eternal, loses its "fear and trembling"—a term coined by Christian theologian and philosopher Soren Kierkegaard—and becomes ripe for sober contemplation by the human intellect.

Such incisive examination of death is eloquently expressed in the well-known poem "Death be not proud" by seventeenth-century English poet John Donne:

Death be not proud, though some have called thee
Mighty and dreadful, for, thou art not so,
For those, whom thou think'st thou dost overthrow,
Die not, poor Death, nor yet canst thou kill me.
From rest and sleep, which but thy pictures be,
Much pleasure, then from thee, much more must flow,
And soonest our best men with thee do go,
Rest of their bones, and soul's delivery.
Thou art slave to Fate, Chance, kings, and desperate men,
And dost with poison, war, and sickness dwell,
And poppy, or charms can make us sleep as well,
And better than thy stroke; why swell'st thou then?
One short sleep past, we wake eternally,
And Death shall be no more; Death, thou shalt die.

To be able to look at death not as something fearful but as an inevitable event programmed by life itself, it is enough to remember that the moment of our disappearance is just as mystical and devoid of apprehension and dread as our appearance in this world, which we take for granted.

Though it may seem paradoxical, death, philosophically speaking, has positive qualities. Death is the greatest healer—when it comes, it unburdens forever those who suffer from the misery of intractable emotional and physical pain and progressive debilitating illnesses. Death forever relieves us of our earthly responsibilities, of painful memory, of guilt and of shame.

Death also serves as the great equalizer of the human race. There is no refuge where people can hide from death. Standing before death, all are equal: the poor and the rich, kings and commoners, the beautiful and the ugly, the talented and the dull.

Why are those who offhandedly deny the existence of God not surprised at how easily and organically the human race fits into the life of this planet? Is it not amazing how effortlessly, and without being taught, very young children learn to sit, walk, run, talk and speak not only one but multiple languages at the same time? Like birds endowed with an intuitive knowledge of their destination when they fly thousands of miles away, we humans miraculously, both consciously and subconsciously, are able to grasp intuitively—who knows, maybe from the previous lives—an infinite amount of information from earliest childhood on, as if it were built into our minds before our birth.

Every moment of our earthly sojourn we are surrounded by the boundless ocean of information and incomprehensible miracles, but we take them for granted and cease to notice them, because we become accustomed to these wonders and because there is an infinite number of them.

For believers, every day of existence is filled with great meaning because life on earth appears to them not as a trivial accident, but as a tremendously important stage in the infinite duration of the life of the immortal souls granted them by God.

Faith in God brings sense to our lives, making them purposeful and precious, dissolving existential anxiety related to the temporal limitation of our bodies. It also serves as a powerful consolation, helping us overcome the tragedy of forever losing our irreplaceable loved ones.

For those who believe existence is a miracle, every moment of life on earth is filled with high meaning and motivation for good deeds based on the firm trust that sooner or later they will appear before God and, in this or another form, will give

Him an account of how they spent the earthly life generously bestowed upon them.

That contrasts unfavorably with what logically follows from the conviction—actually the "religious" faith—of atheists in their proud lack of belief in God. I am well aware that among atheists are countless numbers of caring, compassionate, altruistic individuals; many of them are sincerely responsible toward humanity and the world. However, I believe that without realizing or admitting it they stand on the shoulders of the giants of religious teaching, who have transmitted to society God's ideas of human conduct for eons.

But the inevitable logical philosophical conclusion of the pure atheistic position cannot be any other than that the meaning of life is reduced to *carpe diem*—seize the day. Without belief in the eternal life of our soul, our earthly life functions as pointless vanity and purposeless reproduction of our own kind, with the eventual transformation of the human biological mass into fertilizer for the planet. Indeed, if life is, as a popular Russian song says, only "a flash between past and future," and if, as according to atheists, death is a departure to a complete void, to the vacuum of oblivion, then why should we worry, work, and take things seriously?

My path to faith was prompted by unforgettable life experiences, just as for others who were not born to religion, but who came to it instinctively.

UNDEFEATED FAITH

IT HAPPENED IN THE SPRING, on a bright sunny morning. I was helping my father plant trees in front of our house. As my father planted saplings, I ran to the street's water pump with a watering can. I placed it under the tap, and, after pumping several times with a lever, I filled the can to the brim. Trying not to spill water on my way back, I returned to my father and diligently watered the ground around the seedlings. Meanwhile, my father dug a new hole in the stony ground for the next tree. Our harmonious work was interrupted by a short, old Jewish man with a broad, thick, black beard touched with gray, who appeared as if from nowhere. He wore a black wide-brimmed hat and a roomy out-of-season black coat that was too long for him.

Approaching us, he politely asked my father in Yiddish if we were Jewish. My parents spoke Yiddish at home between themselves but did not let me speak it for fear that I might develop "the Jewish accent," which would allow people to easily identify my "second-rate" nationality. As a result of that decision, I learned to understand conversational Yiddish, but my ability to speak the language was quite primitive.

After my father confirmed that we were Jews, the stranger gave me a long studying look and turned to my father with a question:

"Excuse me, *Reb id*, I can see that you have a good son. Is he thirteen years old already, by chance?"

"No, he is twelve," my father said evasively.

"Oh, but this is very good, *Reb id*. This means that soon it will be time for his Bar Mitzvah."

Traditionally, a thirteen-year-old Jewish boy is considered an adult, is responsible for his moral and religious duties, and must demonstrate his knowledge of the Jewish religion.

My father, a sociable man by nature, replied to the old man's remark with a short "*Yo*"—"Yes"—and in an ostentatious way returned to digging a hole for another sapling.

"And, please tell me, *Reb id*," said the stranger with the beard and black coat, not giving up, "is your son prepared for such an important event in his life?"

"My son does not need to be prepared for anything," my father retorted, no longer hiding his displeasure. "We do not attend any synagogue, and we are not planning to attend one in the future."

"But your son is a Jewish boy," the old Jew objected. "Tell me, who should be taught Talmud-Torah if not children like your son? Listen, *Reb id*, if you wish to prepare your son for Bar Mitzvah, I will be more than glad to help you out. And don't worry about money. I do not do it for money. If you can pay, you pay; if not, that's okay too. What is important is that your Jewish boy is taught Talmud-Torah. That's all."

Without asking my opinion about the offer, my father, a bit more gently, and with an apologetic smile on his face, in a quiet but firm manner once again refused the proposal of the old Jew to introduce me to the world of Jewish religious traditions.

My fate might have been quite different if on that spring morning my father had accepted the proposal of the stranger.

* * *

Despite all the radical efforts by the leaders of the Russian revolution, the Soviet system was unable to kill in people's souls the inner craving for the spiritual, offered freely by religion, but utterly absent in Utopian communist ideas. On the surface, the Soviet Union was an atheistic communist society, but in the bowels of this system yearning for connection with the eternal never stopped because it is a feature of human beings impossible to remove.

During my school years, a classmate, also Jewish, lived not far from me. During summer vacations I spent a lot of time with him. Once when I visited him, his parents were at work, and I noticed on the quilt of their bed a rectangular piece of cloth resembling a scarf. This piece of cloth was decorated with blue transverse stripes and tassels along its short edges.

Next to this scarf-like object was a pair of strange little black boxes with leather straps faded to grey attached to them. These small objects were placed inside larger boxes without straps. On the vertical surfaces of both the inner and outer boxes I could see Hebrew—I learned about that later—letters, which had been almost rubbed away. Perplexed, I asked my friend to explain the purpose of these strange things.

My friend, talkative until that moment, picked up the piece of cloth and the boxes that attracted my attention, quickly tucked them under the large pillow, and then, after thinking a bit, answered evasively:

"Forget it. Don't pay attention to them. I don't even know what they are called. Well, these things. . . " He paused. "My dad puts them on himself when he prays in the morning. Okay? But, please, do not tell anyone what I told you."

It was not accepted to discuss anything positive regarding religion among anyone then, but I wanted to learn more about the objects which I had seen by accident. To learn their intended use took me a long time. Only on the other side of the ocean I found out what the scarf-like piece of cloth and mysterious black boxes were for.

They were *tallit* and *tefillin*, which, in the Torah, God orders men to wear during worship. Putting on *tallit* and *tefillin* is accompanied by a short ritual when a Jew pronounces appropriate blessings.

The Jews have worn *tallit* and *tefillin* during worship services for thousands of years. A *tallit* can be of different sizes, but it should always be rectangular and with tassels (*tsitsit*) at the corners, worn at the shoulders. A worshipper ties one *tefillin* on his arm and places the other on his head. Both leather boxes of *tefillin* contain inside of them handwritten parchments of biblical texts from the Torah. One of them, beginning with the words *"Sh'ma Yisrael, Adonai Eloheinu, Adonai Echad"*—"Listen, Israel, God is our God, God is One"—is one of the most important prayers in Judaism.

I wonder how my allegedly nonreligious parents would react if they saw me now praying with other fellow believers wearing *tallit* and *tefillin* in the morning?

* * *

As I already mentioned, one of the reasons we believe in God is as a logical reaction to the realization of our tremendously humble position within the boundless and eternal cosmos. The dynamics of human society can be compared to the travel of passengers in a slowly moving train: some passengers are comfortably sitting on their seats; others get off the train and disappear, and their places are occupied by new passengers. It is natural for the travelers to be interested in what happens when their turn comes to leave "the train of life."

In the works of the founder of psychoanalysis Sigmund Freud, and in the works of his numerous followers, including anthropologists and psychologists, the wish to meet the Father or God is intrinsic for all human beings. For a number of reasons many people, consciously or subconsciously, try to suppress this natural inner feeling. But even more people are simply unable to suppress it. However hard they try to drown their natural aspiration to search for the absolute, the next moment they realize that they are deceiving themselves.

One of the unwritten traditions of a Jewish family is the determination to give their children the best education they can. From the thousands of years of endless persecution, Jews learned that during social calamities enemies could take away from them everything but knowledge. From my early childhood, my parents repeated over and over again that I must work hard to be a good student. It was done not by coercion but by constant and patient persuasion. For example, whenever we passed by a loader, a digger, or a street cleaner, my father never missed the chance to tell me with a smile that if I did not study well I would have to earn my living, like those people, by hard manual labor.

To tell the truth, there was no need to persuade me to study, since I have always taken great interest in education and treated it with the highest sense of curiosity and responsibility. My nervousness in view of that responsibility reached a crescendo the day before any upcoming exam.

One of the greatest moments of happiness for me—after successfully passing another exam—was to come home with an indifferent expression on my face. It was only when my mother or father anxiously asked me which grade I'd received that I would utter as dispassionately as I could, "Ah, nothing special. An A." This was followed by an always—satisfying moment: generous compliments from my parents.

I knew from books and films that people prayed—but nobody had ever invited or taught me to address God. Despite this, guided by my inner feeling, without any incentives from the outside, before each exam I would find someplace where I could be alone, and there I made my earnest request to God to help me safely sail through another test. Though I was a good member of the Communist youth movement, it did not prevent me from appealing to God to help me gain confidence and achieve success.

My life experiences confirmed this urge to appeal to God in trying times. But even without this appeal to God for help, many times when I faced dramatic events that seriously threatened my life, freedom, or health, at the most crucial moment, when the danger was too close, suddenly another miracle would occur and, as if by magic, the situation would be settled and the trying problem would be solved.

What many people would consider accident or luck, those who believe perceive as another small wonder. Indeed, frequently people say that they owe their special fortune to some kind of an invisible power guarding them. Sometimes such comments produce pessimistic, ironic, or even hostile reactions from many non-believers.

"Come on," they might say with an indulgent smile. "Aren't you a grown-up? How childishly naïve you are! We are nothing more than a little dot in the universe. Whether you believe in God or not, what does He have to do with the individual fate of mere mortals!"

"Yes, we are tiny particles in the universe," could be an answer to such opponents, "but we are particles who can think, feel, hear, and see, who are endowed with consciousness and imagination, which in an instant can transport us—the tiny particles of the universe—thousands of light years away to the most remote corners of the cosmos."

"Man is but a reed, the most feeble thing in nature; but he is a thinking reed," said the famous mathematician and philosopher Blaise Pascal. "The entire universe need not arm itself to crush him. A vapor, a drop of water suffices to kill him. But, if the universe were to crush him, man would still be more noble than that which killed him, because he knows that he dies and the advantage which the universe has over him; the universe knows nothing of this."

The musical strings of the soul of this "thinking reed" resonate to the sight of the divine sculptures of Michelangelo and paintings of Rembrandt, to the sounds of the heavenly music of Bach, Mozart, Mendelssohn, and Tchaikovsky. And if God gave us, His thinking creations, the incredible gifts of life and immortal spirit, nothing prevents Him helping us, His children, to find a way out of the most difficult situations.

In spite of their outward show of rejection of faith, I am sure my parents would have observed the rite prescribed by the Torah for male Jewish infants on the eighth day of my life. Alas, in my case it was destined to happen much later, because I was born on the first day of war, June 22, 1941, in the town of Beltsy, near the Romanian border. At five o'clock in the morning, this town was mercilessly bombed by the German military barbarians, who coolly and mercilessly killed peaceful civilians from airplanes.

My father, who was an army officer, was on his way to the front after leaving my nine-year-old brother in the care of acquaintances, which he and my mother had agreed on. My mother, well aware from my father of the atrocities perpetrated by Nazis against the Jews, left the maternity unit on the third day after my birth, wearing only a hospital robe and a cotton headscarf. Carrying me in her arms, swaddled in a bundle, she went straight to the city *voencomat*—the military registration and enlistment office—and asked the military commissar to help her find her older son. When, with help of the soldiers, my brother was found, she went with both of us to the city railroad station, boarded a boxcar filled with other refugees, and, changing trains one after another, two months later reached the town of Andijan in the Uzbekistan Republic, eighteen hundred miles to the east. There we lived for the next four years, until the end of the war.

After the war, my family reunited with my father and lived in several military communities over the next two years. When my father was discharged from the army, our family returned to the city of Beltsy—the city where my life began.

My father, being an officer, became a member of the Communist Party during the war, but that by no means prevented him from expressing his distrust and contempt—at least at home, when he spoke to my mother—for the official state brainwashing propaganda. Ignoring my presence, he would not miss a chance to utter his anti-Soviet thoughts. Evidently, he trusted that I would never repeat to anyone outside the house what he said, although sometimes he would ask me with a cunning sparkle in his eyes if I would inform on him like the famous pioneer Pavlik Morozov, who betrayed his father many years before to the Communist authorities and was glorified by Soviet propaganda. When I expressed my righteous resentment for his offensive implication, he answered with a friendly chuckle, showing me the absurdity of the idea.

To live a double life—what can be more characteristic of a totalitarian society? Among other aspects of daily existence, such an attitude extended also toward religion.

For example, in my childhood I hardly knew about the Passover holiday. All I knew was that during that holiday Jews had to eat matzah in memory of their departure from Egypt thousands of years ago. Why do the Jews have to eat matzah? According to my fragmentary knowledge, it was because they had had to flee quickly from Egyptian slaveholders and did not have time to bake bread. Those refugees swiftly mixed flour with water and baked the mixture on the burning hot stones of the Sinai Desert. Because officially baking unleavened bread, or matzah, was prohibited in the Soviet Union, Jews did this furtively in private homes whose owners were willing to undertake the risk of such a mission.

Almost everywhere in the Soviet Union during the season of Passover, Jews, loaded with wheat flour they had stockpiled throughout the preceding year, went to such underground homemade bakeries at night to bake matzah for their own families.

In that season the Jewish community of Beltsy would wake up after a year-long hibernation. Already, a week before the feast, Jews—practically openly—discussed among themselves the details of matzah production. When the long-awaited time for action came, the stoves for baking matzah burned from late evening till early morning.

Every year, a few days before Passover, my parents—who always claimed that faith in God was totally beyond their interest and concern—loaded with flour, and leaving me home alone, went for the entire night to bake matzah. They were not at all bothered that they were following the covenant God had made many generations before with the people of Israel. They did not realize that with their actions they were participating in the celebration of an event where the Jews gained their national freedom. Instead, they would say, if asked, that they were simply following the tradition of their parents.

They returned from the makeshift bakery before the sun rose, bringing with them newly baked, still-warm, crispy matzah wrapped in impeccably clean, snow-white pillowcases they had brought from home for that purpose. Their flushed faces shone with pride.

The next day, with unconcealed pleasure, my mother would share with me all the details of the previous night. She would tell me how she and my father managed to find a well-disguised house where the underground bakery was temporarily set up, how they mixed flour with water, how they kneaded and rolled out the dough, then placed it in the oven, and finally took out hot baked slabs of matzah. Then there was always a pause. According to the tradition, long established between us, my mother would wait for me to ask her how they managed to make holes in the matzah.

"Very simple, Vovka. We did them, as always, with a fork. Do not think that it was easy. Really, it was quite a big job," she would say, and then assure me that the next year my father would finally get an item coveted by many Jews—the gear wheel of a broken clock with points around the circumference to make equally spaced holes like those of "matzah made in a professional manner."

Long after Passover was over, we would still be eating matzah prepared by my mother in all possible forms: matzah in soup, matzah fried with eggs, babka with matzah, strudel from matzah meal, and just crumbs of matzah.

Like other Jews, we shared matzah with our Christian friends and neighbors. In a friendly manner, thanking us for the treat, they always told us that Easter bread or *paska* was much tastier than the Jewish matzah.

I asked my father once, "Dad, what does Jewish tradition say about the leader who was in charge of the exodus from Egypt?"

"What difference does it make to you who led the Jews out of Egypt?" my father said, trying to avoid answering my question. "It happened thousands of years ago."

I was not satisfied by that answer and kept asking.

"Okay," my father said after moment of hesitation. "It was Moses who delivered the Jews from Egypt. Why are you interested in that stuff?"

"I just want to know, Dad. Today our neighbors, Uncles Leizer and Yankel, told me that without God's intervention all the Jews would have drowned in the Red Sea and would have never reached the land of Israel."

"What does God have to do with that! Forget about God, and about everything those old men tell you, Vovka. And stop taking interest in such things. Neither your mother nor I are happy with your interest in religion. What do these old people know? Live for today, my son, and forget about the ancient past. Don't you see what is happening around you? Every day scientists discover new secrets of nature, invent lots of useful things, and all *you* are interested in is the useless, obsolete religion. Look at what level of technology our society has reached! Religion has nothing to do with such progress. Remember, we do not need God! We are doing perfectly well without Him."

"I know that, Father. We are told about these things every day at school. But I do not understand: if such a miracle really happened and the sea parted to let the Jews pass, who else might be responsible for that if not God?"

Eventually, my father would put an end to our "theological discussion" and would warn me for the umpteenth time not to discuss such things with anyone. Finally he would leave the room, giving up on efforts to persuade me.

Only many years later did I learn in detail about the miracles of Passover and the special place this holiday occupies in the life of Jewish people.

* * *

I was eleven when I heard for the first time about the Torah and the holiday of Yom Kippur or the Day of Atonement. Next to our house stood a small building, actually a hut, where in the four tiny flats lived four poor families. My childhood friends Avrum and Leika lived in two of these flats. Both of them were two years older than me. During summer holidays we used to spend a lot of time together. Leika's real name was Leah, but everyone called her Leika. Both of my friends' fathers had been killed in the war, and they were brought up by single mothers: Avrum by Feige-Reiza, and Leika by Sheiva.

Because the house had no running water, all the inhabitants, like many other people in that neighborhood, got water from the street water pump, carrying it in buckets. Indoor toilet facilities were out of the question: most of the residents of the town used primitive outhouses.

The apartments where Avrum and Leika lived had dirt floors, the walls were covered with cracked lime plaster, and almost all the window frames were crooked.

Avrum's apartment was in the front of the house, while Leika's was in the back of it. Leika's apartment consisted of a room which at the same time served as a living room, dining room and bedroom for three people—Leika, her mother Sheiva, and Shaindel, who was five years older than her sister Leika—and a tiny kitchen with a small window. The roof of the house was covered with a thick layer of old blackened thatch, and the walls were built from "*lampach*"—unbaked bricks made of clay mixed with straw and horse manure. Nobody remembered when the house had been built. Over time it had settled into the ground, so the door at the back of the house was one-and-a-half steps below ground level. Because of the age of the house, the walls were sagging and swollen outside; for security, they were supported in several places by thick grey boards.

Sheiva had a colorful and unforgettable personality. Poverty had made her haggard and added quite a few years to her age, but her mind was lively and sharp. Her olive-colored face was lined with a net of deep wrinkles; grey strands of uncombed hair always poked out of her old, faded blue kerchief. To tidy hair up requires time, but Sheiva had no free time because she was in a constant fight for daily survival. She had grown up in an exclusively Jewish environment in pre-war Romania, before Moldova had become a Socialist Republic, so her mother tongues were Yiddish and Moldovan, a dialect of

Romanian. Her Russian was quite poor, and she spoke it only when she had no other choice.

Sheiva earned her living by doing small household jobs—mostly by repairing rubber shoes. Her older daughter, Shaindel, was her permanent assistant in this business. Because even a small rain was enough to turn most of the streets in Beltsy—a town situated in the lowlands—into a dirty, impassable muck, high rubber shoes were one of the town's most important and necessary commodities. This environmental factor was responsible for a major source of income for Sheiva's family, allowing them to make ends meet.

When the weather was warm and the wind was gentle, mother and daughter would take their work out of the house into the yard and, sitting on low chairs, surrounded by a pile of galoshes, rubber shoes, and boots, got to work. Preparing the surface of the next pair of shoes that needed repairing, Shaindel skillfully worked with a rasp file, while her mother, first daubing some distinctive-smelling rubber glue on it, neatly placed the patch over the hole in the shoe.

Sheiva had a fascinating, beautiful voice, and everybody in the neighborhood knew about it. Her unsightly and unkempt appearance was totally forgotten when she and Shaindel sang Jewish songs.

Their repertoire was inexhaustible. Most of the songs they sang were sad and are now almost forgotten, but it also contained songs that are still popular today, among them "Tum Balalaika," "Afn Pripechik," "Rojenkes Mit Mandlen," and "A Gleizale Lechaim."

Sheiva sang with a quiet, melodic, heart-touching voice, while her daughter, having inherited genuine musical talent from her, joined her, singing in harmony.

There was a glaring contrast between Sheiva's shabby, faded clothes and the piles of dirty rubber shoes on the ground and her surprising skill to naturally and masterfully express deep human feelings with her singing.

Knowing Sheiva's and her daughter's talents well, people came in droves from all over the neighborhood. The street crowd filled the yard while Sheiva and Shaindel continued to sing, not paying much attention to the listeners and never stopping their work.

But the real feast would begin when a blind musician, violinist Dov Ber, also well known in the neighborhood, joined the "musical group." Before he lost his eyesight as a teenager, Dov Ber helped his father fix bicycles and primus stoves. He went blind when one of his clients brought a broken primus stove for repair and it exploded. It had been filled by mistake with petrol instead of kerosene. Dov Ber, blinded by the explosion, underwent several unsuccessful operations on his eyes. But he did not give up, and gradually he went back to his previous occupation of fixing bicycles. Someone gave him a violin as a present, and, instead of complaining he learned how to play masterfully and how to express his feelings with music.

Periodically, one of my friends' bicycles would break. When this happened, the whole crowd of us went to Dov Ber; none of us wanted to miss the chance to witness nothing less than a circus trick. It was impossible not to admire how thirty-year-old Dov Ber in a tender paternal way touched the broken bicycle with his big hands and, while staring into the far distance with his scarred eye sockets, knowingly, like a medical doctor, examined the bicycle with his smart fingers.

By Dov Ber's emphatic request, we, his young clients, never told him what was wrong with the bicycle, but he was always correct in his diagnosis and, forgetting nothing, without a single unnecessary movement, he quickly and deftly fixed the broken part.

Dov Ber came often to Sheiva's backyard with his violin. Someone always brought him a stool, repainted and repaired many times. He would sit down, draw the instrument to his chin, and play, his violin crying with a human voice, joining Sheiva and her daughter, producing heavenly sounds of joy and sadness.

"Why do we need to go to the theater?" we would ask each other. "Who could play and sing better than our street musicians?"

Once, on a pleasant autumn day, Avrum, Leika, and I sat in Leika's backyard on the grassy, green hillock. It was still quite warm, the birds were singing, the sounds of saws and hammers were coming from a nearby sawmill, and in the distance, as so often happened in the peace and quiet of the small town, we heard the neighbors loudly quarrelling about who knows what.

We had been animatedly discussing the popular film *The Thief of Bagdad* by Alexander Korda, which we had seen a while before, when we heard a loud creaking. It was Sheiva, who, with a visible effort, slowly opened the sagging door of her apartment. When she came out, walking with long, man-like strides, she briskly and vigorously headed toward the place where we were sitting.

In one hand she carried a cackling hen, holding it upside down by its legs, in the other, two old, tattered books with dark-brown leather covers that were worn from age and use. As usual, Sheiva, who was always in a hurry, completely ignored us.

Squatting quite close to us and not letting go of the chicken, wetting her finger with saliva, the woman started to leaf through one of the books until she found the page she wanted and then began to read, muttering the words in a strange language. Curious to know what she was reading, I stretched out my neck and looked at the page over her shoulder. The text had been printed in a language unknown to me. It was really amazing: Sheiva, whose hair was always uncombed, who dressed in simple, cheap, and worn-out clothes, who lived in utter poverty and need, seemed to read and speak a language of which I was completely ignorant.

Then something unimaginable happened: having finished reading from the first book, the old woman opened another and read something from it while energetically swinging the hen by its legs over her head three times. After she put the hen down, she continued reading, periodically mumbling strange words under her breath.

Finishing rather too soon with this mind-boggling, impossible-to-understand ceremony, which we young members of Communist Youth watched with eyes wide open, Sheiva, still totally ignoring us, finished her ritual in a businesslike manner, quickly rose to her feet, straightened her frequently washed, once-black, faded gray skirt, and, taking hen and books, hastily went inside.

"What are those books, Leika?" I asked impatiently, consumed with curiosity.

"Oh, the books?" she responded. "They are holy books. First my mother read passages from the Torah and then prayers from Siddur."

"What language are those books printed in?"

"What language? It's Hebrew," interrupted Avrum, who had been silent until now. "Don't your parents teach you to read Hebrew at home?"

"No, they don't. And what is the Torah?" I asked naïvely.

"You're really something, Vovka, you are!" Leika marveled sincerely. "What do your mom and dad teach you at home then? Aren't they Jewish? The Torah is the book that God gave to us as a guide for life."

"But that is simply impossible," I objected. "You say that God lives high up in heaven. How could He write the Torah there and then pass it to us down here?"

"What's so special about it?" Leika answered with an air of authority, shrugging her thin, dark shoulders. "God can do whatever He wants. If He created everything around us, the stars, the earth, animals, and people, then why can't He do something much easier than that: write the Torah? He wrote it in heaven and then—boom—threw it down to people, and people took the book. Not a big deal!"

Years passed before I learned that, in the narrow sense, the word "Torah" designates the Five Books of Moses, as in "This is the law (Torah) which Moses set before the children of Israel," Deuteronomy 4:44, or "Moses commanded the Torah for us, an inheritance of the community of Jacob," Deuteronomy 33:4.

Meanwhile, in a broader sense, "Torah" means the whole Bible of Judaism. Further expanding its meaning implies distinguishing the Written Torah (Hebrew: Torah She-bi'khtav) and the Oral Torah (Hebrew: Torah She-be-al-pe), the two spheres of Divine Revelation given to Moses on Mount Sinai. In its broadest sense, the word "Torah" denotes the whole body of Jewish law and teachings.

Naturally, Leika, a little girl, could not know then that, according to Jewish belief, the Torah was written by Moses from the words God dictated to him on Mount Sinai. For many years I found Leika's childish, naïve explanation of how the Torah was given to the people quite amusing. However, once, during a hike high in the mountains of California, watching a breathtakingly beautiful sunset, the sight of the boundless, huge, pale-emerald dome of the sky brought me thoughts about God, who presented humanity with countless wonders. Since God could create so many indescribable wonders in the world, then, indeed, if He wished, He could have given the Jews and humanity a guide to life—the Torah—in any way He chose.

Many years have passed, but ever since, on every Yom Kippur, I recall Sheiva, her head covered with a kerchief, strands of grey hair sticking out, lost in meditation and full of determination, and following the ancient Jewish tradition, energetically whirling the hen above her head. Thanks to that remarkable woman, so simple at first glance, so talented in her own way, I learned about the Torah given to the people, and about one of the main Jewish holidays.

A LODGER

MY PARENTS RENTED OUT one room of our house to an elderly couple named Leizer and Pesya Axelrod. Uncle Leizer was thin and of medium height, with a dazzling white, neatly trimmed beard. A heavy smoker, he suffered from fits of loud, wet coughing and was periodically tormented by bronchial asthma.

Uncle Leizer spoke very little and was a serious person, but when something drew him out of his deep thoughts, a warm smile appeared on his face—evidence that he was not only exceptionally intelligent but also quite friendly. He was also an avid bookworm never seen without a book.

When I was ten years old Uncle Leizer saved me from inevitable disaster. In the shed across from our house, my father had set up a photo darkroom where I helped him print black-and-white photos—a fascinating occupation. We did not need an electric lamp with a red filter—instead we had a piece of red glass set into the window in front of the table with the equipment.

One cool day, I decided to stoke a small wood stove in the shed. Naturally, I was not allowed to do so, but I thought that nobody would notice it anyway, so why not to warm up? The shed stood parallel to our house, about twenty-five feet away. On the left side of the house's front door was a simple bench, nothing more than a wide, thick board supported by two small pillars—no back, no armrests.

That day the usual group of people were occupying it: my father and four elderly men from our neighborhood. Uncle Leizer, our lodger, was among them. Uncle Leizer sat on the right edge, so he was closest to the door leading into the shed, where I was trying in vain to stoke the furnace with damp twigs that would not light.

I blew as hard as I could and energetically waved a folded newspaper at the smoldering wood until I lost patience. Not thinking, I grabbed a bottle of kerosene that was used for making fire, opened the two cast-iron circlets fastened to the burner, and splashed the kerosene over the smoking twigs. This was a big mistake. The flames instantly shot up from the burner of the stove all the way to the ceiling, high, hot and out of control. Completely paralyzed by what was going on and still holding the kerosene bottle with blue flames dancing on its sides, I stood in the middle of the shed, not knowing what to do.

This episode could have ended tragically if Uncle Leizer had not come to my rescue. I do not know what attracted his attention; most probably from his seat he saw the reflection of the flames. I saw him suddenly appear in the doorway. If not for his narrowed eyes fixed on the blazing furnace one would think that he was absolutely unstirred. Methodically, without panic, he quickly took off his coat with its white sheepskin fringe and put it over me, covering with special attention the hand in which I still held the burning kerosene bottle.

Making sure that the fire around the bottle was extinguished and that I was out of danger, Uncle Leizer quickly found old rags in a corner of the shed, grabbed them with his thin, old hands and, still showing no sign of panic, calmly covered the flames shooting out of the furnace, putting the fire out.

The accident ended as quickly as it had begun. Once more making certain that everything was okay, Uncle Leizer cast me a final, short, evaluating glance. Then he left the shed with an air of quiet dignity, holding his head high and coughing occasionally.

I was sure that, like all the adults I knew would have done in a similar situation, Uncle Leizer would tell everybody what had happened and would start preaching to me. To my total amazement, that did not happen. Silently joining the others on the bench, as if nothing had happened, Uncle Leizer carefully wiped his face with a handkerchief, cleared his throat, and again lent his ear to the men's conversation. For some time, leaning against the doorpost of the shed, I waited for him to start telling everybody—including my father—what had happened, but this never occurred. Uncle Leizer never told anyone how he had saved me from the fire I started so foolishly.

Seeing that I would not have to explain to my father what had happened and regret my misbehavior, I decided to go, but before leaving I noticed that Uncle Leizer, who was usually serious and thoughtful, glanced at me with a conspiratorial smile hidden in the folds of his mouth. That smile further strengthened my friendship with that elderly man.

After that incident, at least once a day as I passed by the quarters of our lodger, I gently knocked at his door and, receiving a quiet permission, called on Uncle Leizer to say

hello and exchange a few words with him. Most of the time
Uncle Leizer sat at a small table covered with clean, red oil-
cloth, reading different books, one of which he always hid
from me. Once, he was distracted by something, and I had
a moment to see that the book was written in Hebrew letters. I guessed later that it was either the Jewish Bible or a
prayer book.

But the time I really needed visits to our lodger was during school exams.

"Uncle Leizer, I have a written math test tomorrow," I told
him as I entered his room, getting straight to the point.

"So. . .?"

"Uncle Leizer, honestly, this is the most difficult exam I
have ever taken. I just want you to know I am afraid that I
will fail it. . ."

Uncle Leizer did not treat me like a regular schoolboy,
but like a personality. He called me by my Yiddish name,
Velvl. After asking me about small details of the impending
examination and carefully listening to my answers, he became
deeply thoughtful and then, clearing his throat, with a slight
asthmatic aspiration, said in Yiddish: "Good luck. Do not
worry. Everything will be all right."

This was usually followed by a ceremony established
between us. I would walk toward the door, touch the door
handle, and half open the door to go out, when I always heard
the same words of Uncle Leizer that I would miss for the rest
of my life: "*Gott helfen er ich, Velvl*" (May God help you), he
would tell me so eloquently and expressively, as if his blessings
would really be heard in heaven.

Once, I almost closed the door but had not yet heard these
words that I so wanted to hear.

"Uncle Leizer, and what about 'God help you?'" I asked, turning toward him.

Looking at me more intently than usual, Uncle Leizer said softly after a meaningful pause, "God help you, *mein klein kind*, my child."

MEDICINE AND RELIGION

WHEN I WAS GROWING UP, there still existed something that could be called a "cult" of elderly people. It was considered that, since old people had more life experience and human wisdom, younger people ought to demonstrate respect for them. In my childhood and youth, when I vainly tried to find answers to the most important questions facing a human being, it seemed to me that I would be able to find at least a partial solution to the secret of earthly existence if I posed such questions to older people. Such expectation was based on the outward appearance, reliability, confidence, and apparent serenity of those who had reached mature age.

In an attempt to speed up my forthcoming enlightenment, I didn't miss a chance to converse with those "golden age" people, who I, as a child and even as a teenager, believed were close to the ultimate truth. Unfortunately, in time, I realized that such tactics led nowhere. Surprise, surprise: none of the elderly people wished to speak with me about issues of life and death. Moreover, instead of answers to my questions from those who impressed me with their external wisdom, I received reproaches for my idle curiosity. When I lost hope of getting help from adults, I started to look for answers about the wisdom of life in books. Though such books were not easily obtainable in closed Soviet society, I got hold of, read, and reread by all possible means, books written by sagacious and famous thinkers, gradually arriving at the previously unknown but quite expected conclusion that I could never succeed in the quest for the absolute. The more pearls of wisdom I gained from books, the more challenging vistas arose.

Facing that reality, I decided that to satisfy my goal I had to arm myself with patience. I was still young, every day at school I learned many incredible facts from different sciences, I was thriving and steadily evolving while I became older and more clever with every year—sooner or later the moment would come when answers to the tormenting questions about the essence of human existence would reach my consciousness naturally and effortlessly.

Trying to learn more about the laws of nature—a part of which we are—I started to read in large numbers popular books on various branches of science. Countless times I was surprised at how incredibly interesting and fascinating are the new discoveries of the world where we live. Truly fantastic advances in science led me to think that the clues to the mysteries of human existence are in the hands of scientists. For a while, thoughts about God became less urgent to me.

When the time for my higher education came, the question of "what I wanted to become" did not even arise. In the West, young people agonize over their future professions, or how they will "find themselves." The only question *I* faced was what college or university would admit me in spite of my being Jewish. What difference would it make which profession I acquired if each profession offered something unique and interesting? This was well expressed in a line from a popular Soviet song: "Каждый труд у нас в почёте"—Any kind of job we hold in high esteem. The main goal was to get a higher education, which would provide me with a livelihood and give me an opportunity to live a more-or-less independent life.

My future career was decided when, only two weeks prior to the entrance exams, my parents told me that someone promised to help me get admitted to the medical school and, if that happened, consequently, I would become a physician. Until then, the thought of becoming a physician never even once crossed my mind. In the admissions office, my father and I found out, to our surprise, that the medical school consisted of two colleges: one for adult and another for pediatric medicine. Neither I nor my father had a clear idea what sort of animal "pediatric medicine" was.

"Young lady," my father addressed one of the other young applicants, who looked as if she had just come from a farm, "can you tell me, please, what exactly 'pediatrics' means?"

"That means to treat children," answered the young woman.

"Aha. To treat children. That's good. And can you tell me where it is easier for my son to be admitted?"

"What a question. Men do not like to deal with children. Only women apply to the pediatric college, so they are always looking for more men in pediatrics."

My destiny was sealed.

"Vovka, you are going to be a pediatrician, whatever it means," said my father. "Write it in your application and we are done."

Why not treat children? I thought. Aren't they charming?

And that's how I entered the medical field. At that time, I still was unaware that I had pulled another incredibly lucky ticket in the lottery of life: I was to study medicine, the discipline dedicated to learning about the most interesting and complicated phenomenon in the universe, the crown of God's creation: a human being.

The medical school curriculum included a large number of subjects, each of which was exciting in its own way. However, none of them influenced me as thoroughly and deeply as the subject of human anatomy.

For an entire year, I had the opportunity to spend time in the anatomical theater, where, in scrupulous detail, I studied how our human organism is constructed. For me, from the very beginning, anatomy meant an initiation into the deep secrets of nature. A detailed study of the structure of a human body allows a student to perceive the receptacle of our inconceivable "selves."

On all levels of inspection, gross examination, microscopically, and electronically, every separate organ and tissue amazes us with its infinite complexity and perfection. The discovery I made for myself in the process of studying anatomy was that, by virtue of its unquestionable universality and complexity, the human body in a tangible and conspicuous manner, illustrates the fathomless wisdom of its creator. Like no other subject taught at medical school, human anatomy, in every slightest detail, proves the beauty and harmony of the morphological structure of our bodies and the endless perfection of its functions. Moreover, thanks to anatomy I learned that the human race, endowed with a thinking brain, has a special place in the universe.

The miracle of the arrangement of a human body is obvious on all levels of exploration. Even such a prosaic thing as the study of the bone system offers numerous surprising discoveries. The architectonics of the inner part of bones can teach mechanical engineers how to create the strongest con-

structions using a minimal amount of material. Take the temporal bone of the skull: it has an uncannily beautiful pyrami-
dal structure and the most complicated filigree formations,
where, together with the extremely complex organs of hearing
and balance, in a very compact space runs a web of vessels and
microscopic nerves.

All organs and systems, except primary and secondary
sexual characteristics, are common to everybody. For example,
in every bone, even the smallest, with insignificant variations,
there are the same numerous canals and holes to allow tiny
vessels and nerves to run through. This anatomical structure
does not differ in individuals of different sexes, races, or ethnic groups.

Apart from the universal morphology, human anatomy is
a clear illustration of the fact that the complex structure of a
human body does not conform to the chaotic, spontaneous,
unrestricted mechanical presumptions of Darwin's theory
of evolution.

We know the minutest details of the anatomy of the
human eye. On the level of its physiology, we know that
through the optic nerves the visual image, via biological electrical currents, is projected to the occipital region of the brain.
However, science is absolutely unable to provide any explanation of how the external image is, in milliseconds, translated
and interpreted from the electrical signals received by the neurons in the occipital area of the brain to the visual perception
identified and interpreted by the mind.

The human brain is matchless in its architecture and functions. The morphological perfection of this motionless, most
dynamic masterpiece of nature combines with its incomprehensible operational system. We cannot comprehend how the

human brain, the yellowish, jelly-like, medium-density mass has the incredible ability not only to perceive the world of numerous nuances, smells, tastes, and visual objects, but also to integrate and comprehend the received information, and in an instant create visual and auditory images. Besides that, the brain is able to see the world in spatial-temporal dimensions and coordinate the interaction of all organs of the human body with numerous elements of the surrounding world. Despite the seemingly identical macroscopic and microscopic appearance of the gray matter of the brain, every area of the brain is strictly specialized. For example, the frontal lobe is responsible for functions such as judgment, reasoning, problem-solving, and impulse control; the parietal lobe is involved in processing pain and touch sensation, as well as in cognition, movement, orientation, recognition and speech. The temporal lobe is involved in sound sensation, and the Wernicke's area in emotion, memory, and language recognition. The occipital lobe controls visual sensation and processing, and Broca's area of the cerebral cortex controls speech, language recognition, and facial nerves.

Though the product of the brain—the human mind— knows that life ends with death, it also possesses a sense of humor, which helps us to enjoy this transitory life. Of the entire animal world, these characteristics are attributed only to humans.

Darwinists claim that new qualities are obtained by species in order to physically survive. But what can they say about the sense of humor—how does this quality help the species to survive?

If the functions of all five senses could be explained as simply the result of the excitation of a hundred billion neurons and a hundred trillion synapses of the brain, then the matchless miracle of nature, human consciousness, which is capable of processing this avalanche of information, is indeed beyond the comprehension of the human mind. But that is not all. The unprecedented scientific progress of our time is not yet able to offer a single convincing theory that accounts for the phenomenon of thinking. Science does not know how our consciousness creates images, how the material neurons of the brain can, in a split second, form immaterial thoughts that cannot be seen, heard, or weighed; science cannot explain how our brains replicate external objects in our imaginations, how our brains are able to read and perceive those external objects.

The organic structure of brain tissue is made up of ordinary atoms that are not special in any way—namely the same atoms of carbon, phosphorus, sodium, potassium, hydrogen, and magnesium that are usually found in inorganic and organic substances.

When these atoms, which do not differ from other material atoms, happen to be the constituent parts of the human brain, in a mysterious way they become part of the immaterial thinking process—they gain the ability to transform the material world into virtual reality inside of our brains.

Through such incomprehensible capacity, each of us can travel at will to the most remote parts of the universe. These unfathomable miracles of the fluid synthesis of material and spiritual components are taken for granted by people for the simple reason that it happens from the moment of birth and throughout our lives. Science has not come close to decoding the thinking process. The well-known mathematical physicist, Roger Penrose, who is a leading specialist in the study of brain function, believes that in order to understand how the human mind works, it is necessary to approach brain function from the position of a new theory based on the achievements of quantum physics. He suggests that the process of thinking occurs in micro-canals of brain neurons the size of microns and sub-microns.

There is no place for Newtonian determinism where quantum physics starts, which means that the world is interpreted in a statistical and not a purely scientific way.

Among many other amazing natural phenomena, the human brain most conspicuously demonstrates the profound truth known to men of wisdom from time immemorial: behind the apparent simplicity of our world hide the most complicated mysteries of the universe.

Can science claim authority over all knowledge and any questions about existence if scientists, making outstanding discoveries by intuition and the most complicated calculations, have no idea how their brains, which allowed them to make these discoveries, work? Religion lays no claims to the functions and achievements of science; it simply starts where science ends, where problems begin to arise in the perception and explanation of the world.

Our human race occupies the only inhabited planet known to us, which is lost among the millions of celestial bodies of our galaxy, the Milky Way. As the famous theoretical physicist Stephen Hawking puts it in his *A Brief History of Time*, "We succeeded in taking that picture [from deep space], and, if you look at it, you see a dot. . . That's here. That's home. That's us. On it, everyone you ever heard of, every human being who ever lived, lived out their lives. The aggregate of all our joys and sufferings, thousands of confident religions, ideologies and economic doctrines, every hunter and

forager, every hero and coward, every creator and destroyer
of civilizations, every king and peasant, every young couple
in love, every hopeful child, every mother and father, every
inventor and explorer, every teacher of morals, every corrupt
politician, every superstar, every supreme leader, every saint
and sinner in the history of our species, lived there on a mote
of dust, suspended in a sunbeam. The earth is a very small
stage in a vast cosmic arena. . . Our posturings, our imag-
ined self-importance, the delusion that we have some privileged position in the universe, are challenged by this point of
pale light."

If the universe is proportional to the size of the central
railway station in New York, then our Earth will be the size of
a speck of dust floating in the sunlight inside the building.

The mainstream scientific establishment is doing its best
to avoid promoting the names of many accomplished scientists who exhibit a skeptical attitude toward numerous fossil-
ized materialist dogmas. The dissenting representatives of science refer to religion as the final source, the endpoint of the
quest to explain the principles of our universe. One of the best
known among the unconventional "dissidents," Dr. Gerald
Lawrence Schroeder, an Orthodox Jewish physicist, author,
lecturer and teacher from Israel, in his five books dedicated
to this subject, states that there is a harmony between science and religion. From his point of view, which is based on
advanced modern science, religion is not denied but rather justified by science.

In his first work, *Genesis and the Big Bang*, Schroeder convincingly and consistently demonstrates how, considering the
postulates of Albert Einstein's Theory of Relativity, the con-

tent of the first chapter of the Torah, *Bereishit* (Genesis), does indeed accord with the latest available scientific data.

In search of the true explanation of the beginning and existence of the universe, science has offered many different theories, but each of them has been rejected for its incompatibility with common sense, its groundlessness, and illogicality.

Almost all materialist theories suggest that the world in which we live existed always and appeared by itself, without any interference from outside; that extremely complex, organized biological systems, following blindly and spontaneously organized processes, evolved from initial chaos. Finding the truth is the aim of any discussion. Because modern theoretical physics is utterly unable to provide a materialist explanation of how the world appeared, then, by process of elimination, the only way left to explain the emergence of the surrounding world is to accept the premise of intervention by the divine power, which, according to Schroeder, is convincingly presented in the first two chapters of the Book of Genesis.

ABOUT DARWINISM

AN INTERESTED READER can easily find a lot of literature about Darwinism as well as a good amount of literature about how the Darwinian theory of evolution is inconsistent with available contemporary scientific data. According to Darwinists, evolution—free from supernatural influence—through a process of trial and error, over long stretches of time, allegedly creates new species in the biological world. But such belief appears to be a primitive cop-out theory when we look at the strictly organized world of a living cell, in which a great number of synchronous, wholly consistent, and regular biochemical and immunological processes, responsible for maintaining the life of the cell, the organs, and the entire organism, run back to back at astounding speed and in a very complicated manner.

The failure of the theory of evolution is also demonstrated by analyzing countless processes at the level of molecules and atoms integrated into each organ and system of the human body, all of which conform to the laws of nature.

After more than four billon years of Earth's existence, assuming that evolution is the real author of all living things, it would be logical to expect the presence of numerous intermediate, transitional biological species in nature today instead of a limited number of stable morphological and physiological species. However, that is not the case. There are goats and sheep, horses and cows, and not the expected endless intermediate morphological specimens between them. The long process of evolution, confirmed by paleontology and modern biology, has resulted in a limited and not an inexhaustible number of biological species. This can only mean that the process of evolution is not spontaneous, arbitrary, and chaotic, as Darwinists try to present it, but a predetermined plan of the creator.

Naturally, there is no need to reject Darwin's theory of evolution completely. What is important is that evolution has not been the decisive, primary factor in the formation of species and, moreover, has nothing to do with the emergence of life on Earth. The author of the creative power of the universe can only be God, the creator.

The theory of evolution speaks about the survival of the fittest and morphologically best-adapted species but is unable to explain the phenomenon of the human being, who is far from being the strongest in nature, has no fur, shell, or needles to protect his body, cannot fly or run very fast, but is still the most powerful master of the animal world. Despite their helpless bodies, compared to better-adapted animal species, humans are characterized not only by intuitive and responsive behavior but by supreme consciousness, the ability to think and set forth ideas. Human beings, unlike all other representatives of the animal world, live in the past and future as well as in the present and are aware of their mortality. Again, if the features acquired through evolution help species to survive, then why should mankind—the product of evolution, as Darwinists claim—need to possess the awareness of mortality?

Where did our DNA, one of the most complex molecules both in construction and function, come from? Nobody knows. According to the Darwinist theory, fish, through many interim stages of evolution, turned into men. At the same time, nobody can say how fish acquired the genes which eventually, after many millions of years, resulted in a human being.

Which came first: changes in morphology and then changes in the underlying DNA molecular structure under the influence of external factors? Or was it the other way around? What invisible strings and levers connect morphology (visible appearance) with the structure of the DNA molecule (physical structure)?

Modern Darwinist geneticists explain the evolution of species by continuous mutations over eons of time. But numerous scientific data demonstrates that, in the overwhelming number of cases, mutation does not result in the addition of genetic information at the molecular level, but causes defects. Every biologist knows that mutation is not a good thing, but a bad thing. Ask those who suffer from hemophilia, sickle-cell anemia, cystic fibrosis, Down syndrome, and hundreds of other dreadful disorders—inherited diseases caused by mutations.

Another vulnerable point of Darwinism is the issue of sexual reproduction. Let us suppose that a man's sexual apparatus developed as a result of evolution. It would have no function without the simultaneous development of a woman's sexual apparatus. Is it a blind coincidence that two parallel organ systems in nature, in harmony with each other, developed simultaneously?

About a century and a half has passed since Darwin developed his hypotheses, but all that Darwinists can offer in defense of their theory is variations *within species* and not a single convincing case of a transformation from one species into a different species.

Conclusive results of paleontological research indicate that the emergence and disappearance of different species did not occur in a consistent and smooth manner as is suggested by the theory of evolution. For instance, the fossil record has established beyond any doubt that all invertebrates appeared suddenly, as if from nowhere, during the "Cambrian Explosion," five hundred and forty to five hundred million years ago.

There are many more facts that refute Darwin's theory. Take, for example, the infinite complexity of different systems, which can function only when many dozens of required components are available and none omitted. If this is so, then the appearance of numerous complex components should evolve at the same geological time, i.e., simultaneously, but not by the gradual Darwinian evolutionary process. The assumption of spontaneous emergence of regularities from the chaotic evolutionary process is absolutely impossible to prove and is inconsistent with common sense.

Michael Behe, an outstanding biochemist of our time, found and mathematically proved that the biochemical systems responsible for blood coagulation, immunity, and the processes connected with vision are infinitely complicated and cannot be explained by successive evolution. This is another—yes!—scientific proof of intelligent design.

And again, Darwinism—the doctrine of the evolution of living species—does not know how life on Earth emerged.

Many pupils of Darwin are surprised to learn that the founder of Darwinism had himself, more than once, said that his theory was weak. Incidentally, the theory of evolution, asserting survival of the intellectually and physically fittest individuals, or specific group of individuals, became the ideological foundation for Social Darwinism, which Adolf Hitler relied upon when he developed his monstrous ideology that cost so many millions of human lives.

No other creature in nature but a human is endowed with a mind that far exceeds, both in quantity and quality, the minds of the best-developed animal species, including apes, to which Darwin arbitrarily attributes a close relationship to humans.

The human being, endowed with a mind, able to analyze and change his surrounding world in a creative manner, qualities not shared with any other biological species—occupies a special place in the known universe.

ANCIENT RELIGION IN HARMONY WITH MODERN SCIENCE

I NEITHER ADVERTISE NOR HIDE my faith, but on many occasions some of my friends express their sincere surprise at my belief in God and ask me with a condescending smile, "What do you need it for, Volodya? How can you talk about faith in God, dear, when so many incredible discoveries are made daily? Would it not be better to learn more about science instead of praying to God? Do not forget that where science begins there is no place for God!"

Actually, all my life I have tried to stay abreast of the latest scientific achievements. Moreover, contrary to the notions of my critics, the study of religion, along with that of science, has helped me reaffirm my long-established conclusion that strict and uncompromising logic only confirms that science and religion are not antagonists. In fact, they are in complete harmony, supplementing and not excluding each other. Science does not deny the intuitive perception people have about the existence of the creator of the universe; it strengthens that perception.

Despite the outstanding, mind-boggling discoveries of our time, many unprejudiced researchers who work at the forefront of modern science admit the limited ability of science to perceive and explain the essence of the reality surrounding us. Finding no answer to inexplicable phenomena in the field of science, an honest scholar is forced to admit what religion was professing the whole time: God is the author and architect of our universe.

The most perfect mathematical formulas cannot fully describe the laws of nature as researchers of the micro- and macro-world see them. In the epoch of Isaac Newton's classical physics, science described the processes of the material world with mathematical accuracy—where two plus two always makes four. But in modern physics, the phenomena taking place in micro and macro world are described not with mathematical precision but statistically—by equations of the theory of probability—where results can vary.

Materialist science, unwilling to admit before the public that it has lost its supreme imperial position, is reluctant to openly say that the latest research data available in such fields as molecular biology, quantum physics, and cosmology do not deny the existence of God but, on the contrary, *convince* those with a truly critical mind that God exists. Materialists, when facing the unfathomably complex processes of nature, regard them as self-evident, not in need of deciphering, while truly objective scientists, trying to understand what is inaccessible to the human mind, as a last resort, name God to interpret phenomena that science is unable to explain.

Science has no right to claim to be the only available source of knowledge, because it does not study *the origin of an object* but its transformation. Science does not even try to answer the fundamental questions of existence; namely, Who are we? Where are we from? Where are we going to?

Both material science and religion maintain that everything in nature has its reason. And material science arrived at the currently dominating conclusion that the creation of the universe was preceded by the Big Bang. But material science's scientific conclusion was described in Biblical language in the first chapter of the Torah's Genesis thousands of years ago: "In the beginning God created the heaven and the earth." Now, when the cosmological hypothesis of the Big Bang is practically universally recognized by scientists, religion can add that God used the Big Bang in order to create our universe.

Modern science is unable to explain the reason for the Big Bang and has no idea what physical processes occurred during the first milliseconds of the Big Bang.

The famous teacher, Rabbi Moses ben Nahman (Nahmanides), in his commentary on Book of Genesis in the thirteenth century (!), used a Biblical way of thinking incomprehensible to modern readers, to write prophetically that the universe originates from a particle as small as a mustard seed.

Atheists have at the ready two answers regarding the origin of the living universe, and neither of them is satisfactory. The first answer is that the universe always existed. Such statement contradicts current scientific theories, among them the Big Bang as the starting point of the universe and the proven scientific fact that our universe is constantly expanding in space, and, therefore, there must have been a specific time when the process of the universe's expansion began.

The second answer atheists give about the origin of the universe is that the Big Bang theory does not present anything unusual. "Big Bangs," allegedly, are periodic phenomena in cosmology: worlds are created, then they are contracted; i.e., they shrink to the smallest size, only to explode again. This answer is also unacceptable, since it contradicts the laws of thermodynamics.

In the introduction to his other remarkable book *God According to God*, Gerald Schroeder responds to members of National Aeronautics and Space Administration (NASA) who attributed a cause to the creation of the universe. In 2002 and 2007, NASA released a diagram depicting the history of our expanding universe. This information was so significant and fundamental that it led to an award of the Nobel Prize to scientists John Mather and George Smoot in 2006 for their initial research:

> "The origin, our cosmic origin, is described in the diagram as the effect of quantum fluctuations in virtual (nonexistent) space. Before the big-bang creation of the physical universe, before the existence of space and energy, quantum fluctuations were possible. This means that, according to this august body of scientists, the laws of nature, or some aspects of the laws of nature—at least quantum mechanics—predate the physical world. *If they did not predate the physical universe, then the quantum fluctuations that yielded the universe could not have materialized.* The implications of this fact are extraordinary. If time as we understand it is part of the creation, as is usually assumed, then the laws of nature predating the creation must be timeless. They predate time. The laws of nature are totally abstract. They are not nature. They are the laws that will eventually create and govern nature in the universe, once they create the universe by the big bang. *This leap of scientific faith is identical to the biblical posit of a timeless, non-physical creator, God, having created the universe.*" [Italics mine.]

It is typical for atheists to express an amazing intolerance when someone does not agree with their point of view. They either deliberately stop the conversation, or produce a nervous laugh, or resort to outright rudeness. A good example of such an attitude is the offending title of a popular book by the late author and journalist Christopher Hitchens: *God is Not Great: How Religion Poisons Everything.*

Claiming to be absolutely scientifically objective, atheists are trying to avoid constructive discussion by any means, proving with their behavior that in modern times it is not those who believe in God who are irrational, but those who deny His existence.

Even though biological science has made incredible progress, which has made it possible to understand and describe extremely complicated processes on cellular, molecular, and atomic levels, science has not even come close to understanding the origin of life on Earth. There are several materialist theories regarding this issue, but none of them are persuading.

The world famous, Nobel Prize–winning British mathematician, physicist, and astronomer Sir Fred Hoyle wrote in the magazine *New Scientists* in November 1981, "The suggestion that not only biopolymers [molecules composed of long reoccurring chains of small structural units called monomers] but also operational programs of a live cell could have emerged accidentally on Earth, in the primordial organic soup, is surely *absolute nonsense*" [emphasis original].

According to Hoyle, who was a lifelong atheist and Darwinist, this apparent suggestion of a guiding hand left him "greatly shaken."

As is well known, nucleotides (a nitrogenous base, a phosphate, and a sugar molecule) are the basis of hereditary transmission of any kind of information by any living cell. Graham Cairns-Smith, professor of organic chemistry and biology and the author of the book *Seven Clues to the Origin of Life*, says the following about the allegedly spontaneous generation of nucleotides from inorganic elements: ". . . The chance of successful uncontrolled (spontaneous) synthesis. . . of nucleotides on Earth can be expressed by the number represented approximately by a 1 followed by 109 zeros. . . This figure is far more than the number of electrons in the observed universe."

Does the development of the world appear to us random or guided? If it is random, then the truth is on the side of atheists. If guided, then there is need for a God. "The beginning of life," writes Gerald Schroeder, "provides some indication" that development of the world was not random, but guided. "All forms of life at the molecular, genetic level are so similar that it appears that all the life stems from a single origin." It is logical to believe that if even the simplest of microbes are packed with phenomenally complex and extensive libraries of information encoded within their genetic material, then the events to the onetime origin of life were not the result of a fluke but "of an information-filled miraculous cause. . ."

Since materialists are not able to understand how life began on Earth, some of them say that the phenomenon of life was "brought" to our planet by such celestial bodies as asteroids from remote inhabited worlds (the panspermia theory). But this theory only kicks the can down the road. In this case, scientists are simply trying to get away from the true explanation of the origin of life, whether it originated on Earth or some other planet, and suggest accepting their non-scientific conclusion as true. Thus, while science insists on irrefutable arguments about God's existence, when it comes to its own doctrines or theories, it offers unscientific conclusions to be taken on faith.

Another reason the hypothesis that life is imported from space appeals to atheists is that it allows them to reject the special place that our planet occupies within the system of the universe as deduced from Biblical teaching.

However, materialists, searching for habitable planets, refuse to take into consideration that even if traces of life are ever found on other planets, it will not really change the Biblical understanding of the world: God, who created life on Earth, could easily create life anywhere in His universe if He so desired.

Based on the strict criteria of modern scientific research, it has been proven many times that faith in God is neither a whim nor a superstition nor the result of man's capitulation before the fearful reality of death nor a crutch for the neurotic individual.

Faith in God reflects the findings and conclusions of objective scientific data. The results of scientific research in the fields of quantum mechanics, cosmology, and biology (particularly in the field of molecular genetics) cannot but convince us that, along with the material world, there also exists a metaphysical reality, which is not subject to direct perception.

The famous English physicist, mathematician, and astronomer James Jeans, a colleague of Albert Einstein, wrote that science provides irrefutable proof that in all aspects of nature, without exception, we can discover logical and extremely complicated coded information. This information is easiest to trace in the formulas of life, and it is best demonstrated in the study of biological reproduction of even the simplest forms of life.

As for the highest manifestation of life on Earth—the human consciousness—science is unable to provide any explanation regarding the invisible and undetectable dimension which separates brain and mind. The leading scholars working in that field—and most of them do not believe in God—do not deny the possibility that consciousness is a quantitatively and qualitatively different reality than the material structures making up the brain, and that in the elements of nature an undetectable and invisible eternal wisdom exists.

In the last century, changes in physics were so revolutionary that even the great Albert Einstein could not believe that outside the determinism of Newtonian physics extends quantum reality, which is beyond the possibility of being described by the usual equations of classical physics.

Independently from each other, in 1925, Werner Heisenberg and Erwin Shroedinger expressed the view that, as paradoxical as it might seem, a quantum of light behaved both as a particle and as a wave.

Along with that, they established that it is impossible to predict the behavior of a quantum of light with mathematical precision. The only way to describe the quantum of light's behavior is with the help of the theory of probability, i.e., using statistical methods.

Statistical probability, as demonstrated by Heisenberg's Uncertainty Principle, categorically contradicts Einstein's deterministic, Spinozian belief, expressed in his famous phrase, "God does not play dice," i.e., that results of physical processes are definite and not random like the fall of dice. Unlike Albert Einstein, Max Born, Heisenberg's teacher, was comfortable with both the Uncertainty Principle and quantum theory, especially the dual nature of light as both a particle, i.e., matter, and a wave.

Indeed, many contemporary scientists in physics and many other natural sciences are coming to a fundamentally new explanation of reality. It is not religion but science that has proven that a quantum—an element of the material world—behaves too strangely to be considered a material particle: it appears and then completely disappears, simultaneously demonstrating the properties of a micro particle and of a wave, and, therefore, figuratively speaking, in quantum processes, two plus two does not equal four.

In other words, contrary to the fundamental principles of materialism, a material object exists in two contradictory forms—as a particle and as a wave. Thus it is a material and an immaterial part of reality. In the century since the quantum theory was presented, it has been used by scholars of many different disciplines. It serves as an irreplaceable practical instrument in the fields of computer technology, nuclear physics, and chemistry.

Sir Martin Rees, one of the international leaders in the field of cosmology, dedicated most of his life to studying the effects of the primary event of Genesis—the Big Bang. The subjects of his interest were general questions about the makeup of our universe and especially the transformation of the initial chaos of the Big Bang into subsequent order and organization.

Following the theories of Albert Einstein, where $E = mc^2$ (which explains how energy and mass are connected), Martin Rees wondered how the energy of the Big Bang's unfathomable power first was transformed into a formless matter from which billions of galaxies, black holes, stars, and planets were later formed and how conglomerates of atoms transformed, ultimately, into living beings so perfect that they possessed the ability to think about their own origin and destination. After a thorough study of the fundamental laws governing the mechanics of our universe, Martin Rees came to the remarkable conclusion that a deep intimate relationship exists between the world of atoms and the world of stars.

Martin Rees presented his conclusions in the popular book *Just Six Numbers*, where he introduced the six mathematical equations that describe the fundamental relationships between the main elements of the universe. In an objective and forceful way, the numerical results of those equations challenge the doctrine that the universe was created spontaneously from original chaos. These six numbers prove that the universe is based on predetermined and not random relationships, without which the conditions absolutely essential for the generation and further existence of our universe would not exist.

The result of the first equation speaks about the interrelation between the electric power that holds atoms together and the force of gravity between those atoms. Such electric power divided by that force of gravity is equal to ten followed by thirty-six zeros. Scientists have proved that if this number were only a couple of zeros less, the size of the universe would be much smaller than it is.

The second number, E (epsilon), defines how firmly atomic nuclei bind together and how all the atoms on the Earth were made. Its value controls the power from the sun and how stars transmute the primary element hydrogen into the more than one hundred atoms of Mendeleev's periodic table. The value of E is 0.007. If this figure were to be 0.006 or 0.008, we could not exist.

The cosmic number Ω (omega) measures the total amount of matter in the whole universe. If this figure were higher, the universe would have collapsed; on the contrary, if the value of Ω were lower, there would be neither stars nor galaxies.

The fourth number, λ (lambda), was defined in 1998, immediately becoming the scientific sensation of the year. It describes a new, previously unknown, physical force: the cosmic "anti-gravitation" controlling the constant expansion of our universe. In fact, if the number λ were not as negligibly small as it is, stars and galaxies would not exist and cosmic evolution would not have been possible.

The interrelation between the two fundamental energies—the force of gravitation and the energy of mass at rest—is described by the fifth number, Q. Its value is about 1/100,000. If that amount had been smaller, the universe would have been inert and without structure. If the value had been more, there could have been no stars or solar systems. Instead, the universe would include only what cosmologists call black holes—areas where the gravitational field is so strong that nothing, not even light, can overcome it.

The sixth number, D, is equal to three. It has always been known to mankind, because it determines the quantity of dimensions familiar to us. Time is the fourth dimension, but it is qualitatively different from the first three, because it allows inexorable movement in only one direction—forward to the future. If there had been two or four dimensions, life could not have existed. Theoretical physics speaks about the world having at least ten dimensions, but this, like the Superstring

Theory, is just a theoretical supposition not observed in the real world.

All six numbers describe our incredibly complex universe, which started from a particle "as small as a mustard seed" and is constantly expanding, growing at the speed of seventy-three kilometers per second. These six numbers represent a kind of recipe forming the basis for the structure of our universe. If any of the above-mentioned numbers had been different, the existence of stars, planets, and life on Earth would have been absolutely impossible. Science has established with irrefutable accuracy that, magically, each of the six numbers has a strictly defined, not arbitrary, but "given" value, which makes possible the existence of the universe in which we live.

Honest and objective scholars cannot avoid asking themselves the question: are the delicate "setting" and the exact relationships among the values of different fundamental physical forces of the universe a mere coincidence, or rather, do they point to the conclusive proof of God's existence?

There is also another debate between theists and scientists: who created the laws of nature? The extremely complex concepts of the laws of nature, which, nevertheless, can be described by simple equations and numbers, are another demonstration that behind them, inaccessible to the human mind, is hiding an unsurpassed Intelligence.

* * *

Biology, particularly at the molecular level, is another scientific field where materialism is unable to provide adequate explanation of the fundamental processes of the world. The amazing inscrutability of any component of the human body is revealed at the level of a single cell, which is in itself an incredibly complex molecular world, consisting of at least ten million (!) atoms of different chemical elements involved in different organized and purposeful processes. The cell is like a high-tech factory, equipped with artificial languages and decoding systems and memory banks to find and store voluminous information. The reproductive apparatus of a cell is outfitted with lacking error controlling devices, designed to ensure the high accuracy of copied information.

The constructive processes that take place in a cell include the preliminary assembly of a modular three-dimensional protein molecule and the unfathomable ability to make an exact copy of the whole cell in the span of a few hours. Inside a cell, the flurry of activity of numerous components never ceases. Every second, each cell produces two thousand different proteins. A protein is a chain made of several hundred amino acids, each molecule of which consists of about twenty atoms. While you are reading these lines, each cell of your body is selecting about five hundred thousand amino acids made up of approximately ten million atoms, organizing them into previously assembled chains, joining them together, and checking itself by a special process to make sure each chain is arranged in a specific form. After that, the maternal cell in the organ sends the collected proteins to different addresses, both inside itself and outside, to other cellular groups that had previously signaled by various means that they are in need of particular proteins. There are millions of similar miracles that can be told about any cell of a living organism.

Considering the components necessary to maintain the vital activity of a cell—proteins, genetic code, membrane, and so forth—scientifically sound mathematical calculations tested many times cause us to believe that life on Earth could not have arisen spontaneously, without outside help.

In light of the latest scientific achievements, materialists searching for real truth have no right to be indignant when other scientists come to the logical conclusion that God exists. This notion was well expressed by the above-mentioned Israeli scholar Gerald Schroeder: "Since we are not able to give even a rough estimate of the width and magnitude of God's power in the context of the world we live in, the endless prospect of His potential is beyond human understanding."

The basis of unshakable faith in God is not arbitrary imagination, not surrender in the face of the unknown, but the countless attributes of God that people of faith see and live with.

Believers in God, lacking compelling, direct evidence of His existence, have the same logical right to strongly believe in Him as materialists have to disbelieve in Him. Despite the above-mentioned facts of modern science which contradict materialist dogmas, materialists insist on their faith in the "god" of materialism and not the creator. Without doubt, science can successfully explain countless phenomena of the world, but it throws its hands up helplessly when it comes to the philosophical juxtaposition of the infinite ocean of space and time of the universe with the value of a single mortal human life.

A human being does not live in a vacuum but among infinite elements of reality. From time immemorial, philosophers have been trying to answer the question of the existence of the surrounding world: "Why does there exist something rather than nothing? If, as atheists claim, there is no creator of the "something," then who else created the universe where we live?

Who created galaxies and the countless stars they are made of? Who endowed the human race with a mind capable of discussing the reasons for creating the universe?

While atheists, who are proud of their progressive and highly enlightened position, are helpless to give an adequate answer to the question of questions—who created our world?—the answer offered by believers is concrete, simple, and truthful: our world was created by God, the One, who is capable of actions that are beyond human understanding. This logical conclusion does not mean that men should, even for a minute, give up seeking answers to the universal questions of existence.

People are endowed with an infinite passion for exploring and discovering the world they live in. The large number of believers among famous physicists, mathematicians, and inventors during the past millennia demonstrate that, with the exception of limited historical periods when it was in the hands of religious fanatics, religion was not a barrier against the human desire to comprehend the world. Nobody denies the existence of religious fanatics—there are plenty of them—but clerical fanaticism and obscurantism are alien to the majority of believers representing the modern Western religions.

In conclusion of this chapter it is highly relevant to offer another eloquent quote from Gerald Schroeder's *God According to God:*

> "Albert Einstein discovered that matter is actually pure congealed or condensed energy, energy in the form of solid matter. Everything from our bodies to boulders on a mountain is made of the energy of the big-bang creation. The scientific discoveries of the twentieth and twenty-first centuries have gone a step farther. In closing ranks with

the creation, finding that matter and the energy from which matter formed are made of something totally ethereal. In physics we call it information or, more extreme, mind. In the words of the knighted mathematician James Jeans, [mentioned above] the world looks more like a great thought than a great machine. Biblical theology agrees totally, telling us, as we will learn, that God used a substrate of wisdom with which to build the world. This Divine wisdom or mind is present in every iota of the world's being. Divine wisdom was and is present, guiding and forming the way."

THE PATH TO FAITH

IN EXPLAINING OBJECTIVE REALITY, the false religion of
atheism proves its deficiency by refusing to take seriously the
unsolvable limitations of modern science. Categorical rejection of the logical conclusions arising from discoveries in such
fields of science as cosmology, molecular physics, and molecular genetics ironically resembles the indignant rejection and
censure the Roman Catholic Church directed toward astro-
nomical discoveries made by Nicolaus Copernicus and Galileo
Galilei. People who think analytically, who want to be sure
that their faith in God does not contradict the modern level of
knowledge, and who want to know that science and religion
are in sufficient harmony, can find proof of this by becoming familiar with the literature, which is easily accessible,
even though this material is carefully ignored by the official
scientific elite.

Despite all the available scientific background, most people believe in God based not on academic knowledge but on
their natural intuition and a thoughtful, honest attitude to the
endless miraculous diversity of our amazing world, which—
despite its seeming simplicity—never ceases to surprise us
with a continuous kaleidoscope of both big and small miracles. Thoughts about religion cannot escape anyone who has
ever seriously thought about certain undeniable truths: our

humble place within God's creation and our inevitable departure from the wonderful celebration called "life."

One of the most uncompromising atheists of our time, biologist Richard Dawkins, was asked this question: "Professor Dawkins, what excuses will you present to God for your atheism if—despite all your categorical denials of God during your earthly life—after your death your spirit, nevertheless, will appear before the Lord God Almighty?"

Richard Dawkins, never hiding his openly contemptuous and condescending attitude toward believers, gave an answer similar to the one once given by the famous atheist scholar Bertrand Russell—that he would tell God that it was not he, Richard Dawkins, who should be blamed for his atheism, but God Himself. It was not Dawkins's fault that God made it impossible for humans to solve the riddle of the origin of His universe and made proving His existence so difficult.

However, God would not be right to accept such a cynical excuse. He will look at Dawkins with His all-seeing eye and probably will say to him something like this: "How is that so, Professor Dawkins? You were given a perfect mind and five excellent senses. I endowed you with talents so you could become a famous scholar and a popular writer, and look at you—despite your outstanding intellect, all you were able to accomplish was rejection of the one by whom you were created. You, representative of the crown of my creation, refused to recognize me who filled your world with a cornucopia of manifestations of my presence. How could you, a shrewd and observant scientist, fail to notice the countless proofs of my presence? How could you fail to become aware of me in the sensation of beautiful fragrant aromas, in the rainbow of wonderful tastes of food, in magical sounds, in dizzying visual images, in the mystical colors that surrounded you, in the touch of a child's hand, in the soul-uniting glances of your dear ones, and in the inner trembling imbedded in your heart which you could not avoid experiencing when your mind reached the highest peaks of your consciousness?

"How could you—a man of modern science—fail to see my presence in the organization of a single atom, in the structure and behavior of molecules, in the makeup of the building block of life called a cell, which was so close to your profession, and not least, when you gazed at the night sky studded with countless stars and galaxies? You were a world-recognized scholar, yet for some reason you refused to be illuminated by my infinite wisdom on your path to understanding the earthly world.

"Tell me, Dawkins's soul," God will conclude with a sigh, "after all, you were not blind during your earthly life. Could you not notice *anything* that would appear divine to you down there, from where you just arrived?"

In one well-known parable, a believer is a victim of flooding. The water level rises rapidly, causing him to climb onto the roof of his house. A boat comes by and offers him help, but the believer proudly states that merciful God, whom he prayed to and served all his life, will prevent his destruction and soon will come to his rescue.

Time goes by, the water rises, and another boat passes. The people in it urge him to get in, but he refuses, proudly saying, "I am a man of faith. God will save me."

When the water is around his ankles, a helicopter flies over and drops a rope ladder. Again, the man turns down his rescuers and shouts up to them, "I am waiting for God to save me!"

The water keeps rising, and finally the believer drowns.

Now, he stands before the throne of God and bitterly complains:

"Almighty God! Is this fair? You know my love for you. Three times a day and more I offered you prayers. I dedicated all my life to your service! Tell me why did you not save me; why did you forget your faithful servant?

God answers, "Who told you that I forgot about you? I sent you two boats and a helicopter. Is it my fault you kept declining my help?"

In addition to the above-mentioned six numbers that describe the basis of our universe, scientists have uncovered much more evidence pointing to the fact that we do not live in a world of chaos but in a world of established order and laws.

Take for example the position of our planet, Earth. Compared with other celestial bodies, our blue planet is ideally located within the Milky Way galaxy, which, in combination with thousands of other so-called coincidences, makes the home of mankind amazingly well adapted to sustain life.

Anyone curious and open-minded about the organization of nature is sure to be awed by the perfectly elegant and intriguing mathematical formulas describing the laws of nature, laws of complex physical and chemical processes, and geometric and trigonometric theorems.

The assertions of atheists that the reality around us was created out of chaos and that the clearly defined organization and harmony we live in are the result of a natural cosmic evolution contradict the basic principles of physics: according to the laws of thermodynamics, without additional energy, chaos becomes even more chaotic.

Unable to explain how the universe originated, atheists continue to claim that what believers call the miracle of creation is actually the result of a series of accidents. They categorically refuse to contemplate that the aesthetic beauty, purpose, and ideal organization of nature might be a result of external intervention, of intelligent design.

For a believer, all the splendor of our reality was outlined by the invisible hand of providence.

For an atheist, the beauty of mountains, the fascinating smile of a child, the perfection of a flower, and the astounding complexity of the human eye are just facts of life.

What seems to atheists nothing more than an elementary combination of coincidences is to believers the testimony of a divine presence in everyday life. The human race lives not in a world of chaos and absurdity, but in a world where order and regularity reign, where mathematical, physical, and chemical formulas describing the most complicated natural phenomena amaze us with their seeming simplicity. A careful and objective observer will surely come to the conclusion that behind the seeming simplicity of the ordinary events occurring around us hides an unfathomable complexity—evidence of the presence of the Great Mind.

Let's look at the idea of the author and creator through the eyes of people who are far from science, the millions of people who breathe the air of our incredible blue planet, whose souls are touched when in special moments of their lives they encounter the face of eternity. Can one find words that fully express the ocean of feeling experienced by parents at the sight of their child's happy smile or the emotional harmony of lovers when they look into each other's eyes? No words can express the inner music that sounds in people's hearts when they encounter the magnificence of nature, the canvases of great painters, or the immortal works of great composers.

Those who never have an opportunity to become familiar with cosmology, molecular physics, or genetics find proof of the divine presence in numerous episodes of their lives and in every element of existence. For them, the presence of God does not require scientific proof; they perceive Him with their whole beings, feeling His invisible hand safely steering the wheel of the universe.

HOW I WAS A TEACHER OF
SCIENTIFIC ATHEISM

IN THE SOVIET UNION, where religion was continuously repressed, people seldom shared their personal opinions about religion, but once I found myself in a situation where I could not avoid giving a more or less straight answer about my attitude toward the idea of God.

In September 1971, the local trade union committee of the Odessa Infectious Diseases Hospital, where I worked as a physician, put me in charge of the Scientific Atheism Study Group for nurses and hospital attendants. Considering the possibility of undesirable consequences, I could not turn down such an offer, however unattractive.

In spite of the fact that the conclusions of modern science in the fields of cosmology, nuclear research, biology, and mathematics demonstrate that religion can explain the fundamental bases of the universe better than science, in order to gain more authority, atheists call their "science" concerning the absence of God "scientific atheism."

After giving some thought to the matter, I found a way to teach scientific atheism that allowed me to avoid compromise with my conscience.

At that time in the Soviet Union, the book *Bible for Believers and Nonbelievers*, written by Polish writer Zenon

Kosidovski, was published in great quantities and was widely available. Even with the semi-legal position of religion in the USSR, interest in religion never faded, so Kosidovski's book, one of the rare literary publications to successfully survive the censorship of high party officials, became an instant bestseller. Up to this time I believed that this work must have been a dissidents' Trojan horse somehow allowed to become a part of the official materialistic propaganda.

In his *Bible for Believers and Nonbelievers*, Kosidovski first describes in detail the contents of the Bible but then, in a professorial manner, rejects its content, showing that the Bible is incompatible with common sense.

Because it was mandatory for the study group members to attend, or, more exactly, as we used to say in Russian, to be present on a "voluntary-compulsory basis," and because absentees in the Soviet system could be punished in various ways, the attendance of the study group was close to one hundred percent.

An additional reason for the "popularity" of the study group was that the classes were conducted during working hours. Under such arrangement, nurses and nurses' aides came to the meeting hall of the hospital every Friday at 2 p.m., "thirsty" to learn what scientific atheism said about the "non-existence" of God. Naturally, while the study group discussed the lofty topics of scientific atheism, the patients in the hospital departments remained in their rooms unattended, enthusiastically hoping for God's intervention to relieve urgent problems with their health.

"Dear comrades," I began, with Zenon Kosidovski's book in my hands for dramatic effect, "to be more effective and convincing in our atheistic work we must learn how to criti-

cize unenlightened and retrograde believers in the most effi-
cient and skillful manner. With this in mind, we should edu-
cate ourselves in what religion tries to say in order to brain-
wash people."

Thus, the method I chose for teaching became an introduction to the content of the Bible for my audience.

I did most of the talking. There were practically no questions, because the minds of those in attendance were too busy
with thoughts about their official and domestic duties to allow
them to actively engage in discussion of the presented material. In addition, some of them were so tired that they spent
the entire hour with their eyes closed.

We had reached the middle of the Book of Deuteronomy,
when out of the blue came a political inspection. On that day,
unbeknownst to me, a representative from the district party
committee was among those who attended the study group.
Her mission was to check my qualities as an instructor of
atheistic education.

"Were you ever trained how to teach, doctor?" she asked
me, with a severe maternal reproach in her voice, when we
were left alone in the room. "I can see that you use a book
approved by the party as a reference, but, as a teacher of scientific atheism, you must be more careful with the material that
you present to your students.

"We expect much more from you," she continued.
"Nobody needs to hear about the Moseses, Isaacs, and phar-
aohs at all. First of all, they are not our people, and secondly,
this is totally useless information. Who cares? People do not
understand you. Your main function is to drive into the heads
of your listeners the idea that religion is the opium of the people. So, instead of quoting what Abraham and Moses said, you

should present the ideas of Karl Marx, Friedrich Engels, tell them about Engels's book against Dühring, about Vladimir Ilyich Lenin, and, most importantly tell them what our party says about religion. You should define religion as a class enemy, because religion distracts people from building socialism. Is that clear to you?"

"I will definitely consider your advice, comrade," I promised solemnly.

"Very good. Please don't forget that we will check on you again. Without warning! Be ready!"

In my experience, this kind of inspection was a mere formality, and I knew that this party official would never come to my class again. So we safely used the teaching method I had chosen until the end of the academic year. Through the course of teaching it, I became better acquainted with the contents of the Bible, which was officially banned and strictly forbidden for publication and distribution, and I better understood its place in our civilization. I hope that my listeners did not waste their time either.

ABOUT JEWISH IDENTITY

HUMAN CHARACTER IS INFLUENCED by two main factors: heredity and environment. Both these factors play important roles in defining personality and determining connection with the destiny of the nation to which the person spiritually belongs.

Starting from around the age of six and until the last days of my living in the former Soviet Union, frequent encounters with direct, unvarnished anti-Semitism were unavoidable occurrences in my daily life. It was a sad irony that I experienced the most vivid demonstration of undisguised ethnic hatred and scorn when I studied at a bastion of the most humane profession—Kishinev Medical School. There, practically daily, a small number of students openly expressed their hostility and hatred towards the Jews, both verbally and physically, reminding their Jewish classmates that they were collectively responsible for all human problems.

From a young age, I made a firm decision to use for my own benefit attempts to offend and humiliate me as a Jew. I used them to temper my own character, to learn to behave not as a victim but as a man who does not heed what ill-wishers say.

Moving to the free world and having access to the vast literature about the history of anti-Semitism—something that was completely out of reach in the Soviet Union—I was able to fully realize how deeply this particular ideology of hatred has been absorbed into the mentality of the world. Since ancient times barking, vociferous accusers have used the Jewish people as scapegoats for the accusers' own sins and shortcomings. Eventually, I came to the conclusion that anti-Semitism is a political weapon: when it fully exhausts its ugly, false accusations against the Jews, it will stop at nothing to harm them by ideological and physical means.

As might be expected, anti-Semitism was an important factor in determining my place in life. The only decision I could possibly come to was that, as long as that ugly ideology exists, it is my moral, religious, and historical duty to be with my people. Not to do that would be a betrayal—betrayal of thousands of years of hallowed tradition and of the memory of victims of crusades, pogroms, the Holocaust, and countless other tribulations suffered by innocent people.

Gradually, I realized that the Jewish people are not only an ethnic group with a specific history and culture, as I thought when I lived in the Soviet Union, but are mainly identified by the religion they hold in common, based on the written and oral Torah given to Jews during the Divine Revelation at Mount Sinai.

In the Soviet Union, where material about Israel was subject to state censorship, any information disseminated about that democratic, proud, and brave country was imbued with hatred and disdain. Judging by the huge number of newspaper and magazine articles Soviet propaganda published against "a little sliver of land," the tiny State of Israel, to the outside observer this country appeared to be a superpower serving as the sole obstacle to global peace and co-existence.

The pervasive anti-Semitism and the purposeful campaign against Jews and the Jewish state, which were methodically conducted by the Soviet government in the past, still exists in different forms in the territories of many former republics of the former Soviet Union.

The majority of Jews who lived in the USSR were exposed to unrelenting persecution and felt like second-rate citizens. They knew of the existence of the State of Israel but avoided talking about this legitimate state so as not to be labeled Zionists. Behind the Iron Curtain, the State of Israel seemed to Russian Jews to be an unrealizable abstract notion.

For me, Israel became a tangible reality when one of my schoolmates, Boris Plotnik, immigrated together with his mother and her sister to the young state. His father, a submarine sailor, had been killed during the Second World War.

Boris was a good student. Although he was short, he was one of the best athletes in school. We lived rather far from each other but met quite often. In 1953, out of the blue, without going into details, he told me that very soon he was moving to the State of Israel for a family reunion. I was astonished, because it was well known that the Soviet Union hardly ever freed its citizens from its "passionate love embrace."

At Boris's request I went to see him off on the day of his departure. We got to the station long before the train arrived and waited outside on the homely platform of Beltsy North Station. I knew nothing about the country where my friend was going, so I tried to ask him, but he did not seem to know anything himself.

The train, slowly puffing out thick smoke from a pipe on the top, arrived at the station. I shook Boris's hand as he was preparing to board the railroad car, but then his mother, who I thought was not paying attention to us, interrupted:

"You guys will never meet again, so you had better give each other a good hug at parting," she told us. "Borya is going far away and forever."

We agreed to write to each other, but we never did.

The train started off. Waving, I ran along trying to catch up with it until the platform ended. From the open window of the car, I saw Borya Plotnik who happily waved back to me.

My friend's departure heralded an important change in my life: for me, the State of Israel was transformed from an illusory symbol into a real existing country. Shutting my mind against the unceasing stream of official anti-Israeli propaganda, I began to understand that this amazing country existed where, unlike the place where I was born and lived, Jews were not uninvited guests but full-fledged citizens.

Many years later, during my first trip to Israel, I tried to find my schoolmate with the help of telephone directories and friends but without success. It was some years later that I heard the sad news from a mutual friend.

"Don't you know yet?" he was surprised. "Borya is not alive, unfortunately. I visited his mother many years ago. She told me Borya was in the IDF force, rose to the rank of major, and was killed in the 1982 Lebanon war. Recently, in the newspaper, I read that in Tel Aviv they named a street after him."

After Boris Plotnik's departure in 1953, I heard only fragmentary news about Israel until, when I was in my last year of medical school, I had another opportunity to learn much more about that amazing country.

My classmate, Lilia Zaidman, who lived with her husband and parents in downtown Kishinev (now Chisinau), invited me to her birthday party. In her apartment, on the desk, I noticed books and brochures printed in Russian and

Hebrew. I browsed through them and found out that these brochures were about different aspects of life in the State of Israel. Lilia explained that her Israeli relatives recently came from Israel for a visit and brought that information to her.

I seized the rare opportunity to get acquainted with life in Israel, which was so unfamiliar to me. I learned that, while the Soviet Union boasted about its internationalism at the same time it regarded Jews as second-class citizens (or, as Yevgenia Ginzburg wrote in her book *Harsh Route*: "representatives of a mysterious tribe of the people's enemies"), in Israel, over recent years, Jews managed to successfully develop a rich cultural and social life. I also realized that, unlike in the Soviet Union where Jews were categorized as people of questionable loyalty, in Israel there seemed to have been reborn a Biblical Jew, who was not ashamed of his origin but, on the contrary, was proud to belong to the only ancient nation on earth that—after two thousand years of Diaspora—was able to revive its state, culture, and modern language, to turn a land of deserts and marshes into a blooming garden and to make it the center of Jewish religious and social life.

Instead of anticipating another personal insult for being Jewish, as they would have in the Soviet Union, the Jews of Israel regarded themselves as equal among equals, full-fledged citizens of the family of nations, with the same right to respect as any other nation of the world. In Israel, former Soviet Jews joke that in the Soviet Union "dirty Jew" was a typical daily insult, while if a fellow Israeli calls them "a dirty Jew," they know that it is time for them to take a shower.

In the Soviet Union, official propaganda tirelessly hammered disrespect toward Jews into the minds of the masses. Both Lenin and Stalin refused to consider Jews as a nation. In their view, Jews could only be identified by some ethnic customs and by their "reactionary" religion. How could the Jews consider themselves a nation, wrote Stalin in one of his works, if Jews in Russia as a national group did not even have "a direct access to the sea"?

The literature I got access to at the home of my classmate from Kishinev became a very important landmark in my liberation from slave mentality. It took many more years before I finally got rid of the feeling of national and personal inferiority that official propaganda continually imposed on me from childhood.

Learning about the ancient and modern history of the Jews who lived in Russian territory from at least the tenth century and the disproportionately large contribution Jews made to the science, culture, and economy of Russia, I became more and more convinced of the injustice of the label "uninvited guests" bestowed on my people by the Soviet propaganda machine.

Finally liberated from the last remnants of the mentality of someone who was not born to be free, I was able to understand the deep meaning of the words of the prophet Isaiah (60:2–3), words that before were impossible for me to understand: as a Jew, I had a right to take pride in the honor of belonging to my people, whom God gave the greatest responsibility to observe His commandments and to be "a light to the nations."

My closer acquaintance with the Torah and classic works by Jewish and non-Jewish authors played an important part in this transformation. In my former homeland, I did my best to avoid conversations with those who did not hide their hatred towards Jews. However, avoidance was not always possible.

About Jewish Identity

When my opponents ran out of their schizophrenic arguments to justify the vilification of Jews, they played their trump card. I have been personally accused that two thousand years ago—fifty generations or more before I was born—my ancient ancestors allegedly crucified the Jewish rabbi, Jesus of Nazareth. No arguments refuting the absurdity and unfairness of such accusation had any effect on my accusers. My crude prosecutors handed me the sentence with no right to appeal. Gradually, I succeeded in cultivating a sense of emotional immunity toward insulting and undeserved remarks regarding something I had not chosen—my parents, my national belonging.

In Odessa, where I lived with my family until 1970, the only functioning synagogue was situated far from downtown in a suburb called Peresip. None of the Jews among whom I lived went there and none expressed their regrets on this subject.

Families of professionals of my social stratum lived from paycheck to paycheck. In order to support a family, one had to work extra hours at more than one job. I did plan several times to visit the remote Odessa synagogue but could never find the time. The other reason for hesitation was the well-known fact that KGB informers always hung around religious institutions and nobody wanted to be put on the list of untrustworthy citizens and face the risk of losing a precious job.

FROM ODESSA TO CHICAGO

THANKS TO ALL KINDS of heroic efforts by Soviet dissidents and by Jewish and non-Jewish Western activists to attempt to influence the government of the Soviet Union, a historical miracle took place: Jews were allowed to leave the state that had not yet succeeded in becoming an embodiment of the socialist dream. In 1974, the Soviet government let its Jewish citizens leave the country without paying the enormous education tax. For Soviet Jews, the possibility to practice their religion without being persecuted and having their human rights violated finally materialized. It would have been unwise to miss such a great opportunity, so without delay we applied for permission to leave the "communist paradise."

As for so many other emigrants, the main reason for the Soviet Jews to leave their homeland, where they were born and where their ancestors lived for hundreds of years, was their desire to live in a country where they would enjoy political, economic, and religious freedoms.

After arrival in the West, new immigrants live through a very difficult period in their lives: they have to learn a new language, get accustomed to the lifestyle of a new country, and determine the future of their children. Not least important for them is also to return to their prior occupations or to start new ones in order to provide for their families.

To continue my professional career in pediatrics, which before my arrival in the US. I had practiced for more than ten years, I had to take qualification tests for foreign physicians, complete residency training, and then pass many other professional exams.

New immigrants, or as we are still called in this country, Russian Jews (Russian nationalists almost faint when they hear that the "noble" Russian people can be in any way associated with the Jews who are so despised by them), were offered various charitable aid, except for one significant omission— they were given no help in understanding this country's religious life.

When Russian Jews began to arrive in Chicago, the common talk in all the synagogues of the city was about the importance of helping them. In Reform, Conservative, and Orthodox synagogues, rabbis urged their congregants to take care of the immigrants and help them to get absorbed into a new society. In real life, only a few synagogues, mostly Orthodox, offered practical help to immigrants in understanding the Jewish religion, organizing weddings and Bar Mitzvah ceremonies, finding jobs and accommodations, learning English, and providing support to the elderly. Since we lived far from these synagogues, it took some time before we learned of their existence.

In the meantime, we had interesting encounters with different Christian missionaries who wanted to convert us to Christianity. While most of the Jewish religious organizations of Chicago vainly waited for new Jewish immigrants to find and visit *them*, a small number of Christian organizations in the city did their best to convert the newly arrived Jews to their religion. By different methods, they found out the whereabouts of Soviet newcomers and then contacted them to guide their "unenlightened souls" on the right path.

For my family, born and brought up on the other side of the Iron Curtain, moving to the West was tantamount to traveling to another planet. Among other numerous, incredible things, we were happy that, instead of living in our former communal apartment, where the kitchen and toilet facilities were shared by five families—two representatives of which were aggressive alcoholics and anti-Semites—we, as if by magic, were able to live like humans. Just imagine: we had our own separate, comfortable two-bedroom apartment to live in! Those who have had an experience with communal apartments will vigorously confirm that just the possibility of living without other people violating family privacy would have been a good enough reason to leave the Soviet Union and come to the amazing United States—a country whose incredible attributes so many people take for granted. It was only a pity we were not able to come here sooner.

We intentionally settled down in a "project"—housing for low-income families—to experience first hand the process of going through the melting pot from which the legendary America starts. Needless to say, it was helpful financially as well. Quite soon, my wife managed to find her first job as an office secretary in a large insurance company. While I worked hard preparing for medical exams, she was earning a scanty salary, but we were very, very happy.

RELIGIOUS DISPUTE

ONE MORNING the telephone rang in the kitchen of our project apartment. A strange young man, speaking broken Russian with a strong English accent, greeted me politely, saying that he had obtained my telephone number from the local Jewish organization. He had called there to volunteer to help Russian refugees in the best traditions of Christianity. Besides this, he was learning Russian at Wheaton College and now wished to improve his Russian through language exchange. He suggested that I teach him Russian, and he would give me lessons in English.

In reverse translation to English, his Russian to my ear sounded something like:

"You knows, I think, to you and to me might be its veryee good taught you me and I you mothers' tongues. Excuse me—I not sure exacktlee—you will to learn of English and me of Rooshian. To you OK, to mine OK. How to look out at my offering? Byootifool."

At that time my main goal was to pass medical exams and each minute really mattered to me, but I could not refuse the attractive offer—to learn colloquial English with a native speaker.

So deciding to make time and thanking the stranger in advance, I immediately agreed to the proposal. The young man was so excited to hear that I accepted his offer that he said he would come to me at once; somehow he knew my address. I found it a bit strange that he did not ask if his visit would be convenient to me, but I thought, "Anything is possible. Maybe this is normal for this country."

Very soon, David—the name of my visitor—appeared at my door. He was a medium-height, thickset, thirtyish young man with an honest and open face that radiated the inexhaustible enthusiasm and energy of the American pioneers. He carried a brown suitcase.

Expressing great delight at our meeting, David shook my hand for a while, repeating many times how pleased he was to meet me.

I hastily prepared tea for us and put the Maria biscuits on the table and soon, peacefully talking like two old friends, we were sitting at the old table in the living room, which was furnished with odd second-hand pieces of furniture, some of which were given by our new friends and some that were just alley castoffs.

Since we had decided to exchange languages, I tried to speak Russian. At first David answered enthusiastically, but soon it became clear that his knowledge of spoken Russian was even poorer than my English. After twenty minutes of attempting to speak Russian, David gave me a charming smile and suggested—only for this session—to communicate in English. He was impatient to discuss some burning issue with me.

"Vladimir," he addressed me in English, "do you mind if I ask you a personal question?"

"Of course I don't! I'm all attention, David."

"Tell me, please, do you believe in God?"

"How is it possible to have no faith in God?" I answered promptly, glad at the unexpected opportunity to share my opinion on that issue with my visitor. "I do believe in God. And what about you, David, do you believe in God?"

"Not only do I believe in God, I also want other people to have faith in Him as well," answered David, obviously emboldened by my answer.

"In that case," I said, "this means that we hold the same views. For me, the existence of God is so evident that I can't stop wondering why so many people do not believe in Him. I know this may sound naïve, but I'm sure that everyone who just breaks away from the vanities of everyday life for a while and honestly tries to think it over will inevitably come to the idea of God."

"I absolutely agree with you!" cried my companion happily. He finished eating his biscuit and, moving aside the teacup, continued, thoughtfully, "Just as you do, I feel that God is always with me. I accept Jesus Christ as my personal Savior. Jesus Christ is always with me. We should be indebted to him forever because he gave his life to redeem us from our sins!"

"Just a minute, David. Unfortunately, our ways part here. I respect you, I deeply respect your religion, but our opinions about Jesus differ," I interrupted. "But, please, do not take it as any kind of offense. You are a Christian and I am a Jew, and, naturally, we hold different views on the subject. The main thing is that we are not atheists, but believers. We both trust in God. You also believe in Jesus Christ and the Holy Trinity, while I believe in the God of Abraham, Isaac, and Jacob as described in the Torah or, as it is also called, the Pentateuch, written by Moses, which Christians call the Old Testament. But that does not make me respect you and your religion any less; what really matters is that any religion should motivate people to practice goodness in their lives."

David listened tensely to my appeal for mutual tolerance and respect. Judging by his expression, a talk about the difference between Judaism and Christianity was not of any interest to him. He was impatient to move back to the subject that, it became more and more obvious, was the real reason for his rushed visit.

"Of course, I know that you are a Jew, Vladimir, and I'm really glad that you take an interest in religion," he said at last, cheering up. "I believe in Jesus Christ with all my heart and soul, and as I follow his precepts, I consider it my moral duty to fulfill his will and save you. Only through faith in Jesus Christ and his mission on Earth is it possible for a man to obtain salvation and eternal life. You cannot deny, Vladimir, that God sent us his only son, Jesus, to redeem mankind from its sins—including those committed by me, by our friends, and by you!"

"Let me give you my honest answer," I said. "As a Jew, I do not feel I need a mediator between myself and God to receive forgiveness for my sins. When I pray, I speak directly to God. The God I believe in is eternal and One. To obtain redemption from my sins as a Jew, I need no mediators or defenders, including the great teacher, Jesus of Nazareth. As for salvation, this concept has no equivalent in Judaism. Salvation from sin is unnecessary in my religion, because the Jews do not believe that mankind is inherently evil or sinful or that it is in need of Divine Intervention in order to escape eternal damnation.

"Look, David, if faith in Jesus automatically redeems you from any possible sins, then how does it prevent people from committing new ones? Suppose it is possible, God forbid, for the killer of an innocent child to be saved by faith in Jesus. Will such a salvation resurrect his victim from the dead or will it somehow diminish the suffering of his living parents? Daily, in their prayers, religious Jews ask God to forgive their sins, and on the Day of Atonement, like one big tribe, they again ask God to forgive the sins they have committed before Him and against His commandments. Not only with prayers, but also with their actions, the Jewish people hope to earn and obtain absolution of their sins. And for specific offenses against a fellow human being, Jews ask forgiveness directly from the affected person on the Day of Atonement."

"Well, no question, you are a well-read man, Vladimir," David interrupted me. "What you say about the absolution of sins is interesting. I am not an expert in comparative religions, but, in any case, you should not forget that without the participation of Jesus Christ complete absolution of sins is impossible. And now tell me just one thing: can you deny that Jesus Christ is the Messiah?"

Before answering David's question, I thought to myself how great it is to live in a country where citizens, without losing respect for one another, have the precious opportunity to discuss, on an equal basis, freely and peacefully, their opposing views.

Only recently, I could hardly find a Christian in Russia to whom I would say that Judaism, which evolved almost four thousand years ago, has the right to respect, just as other religions do, especially for being a religion that preceded two other great monotheistic religions, Christianity and Islam, by millennia.

"Judaism and Christianity interpret the doctrine of the arrival of the Messiah in different ways, despite the fact that

our religions have much in common. Actually it is the princi-
pal difference between our religions," I began. "Judaism does
not believe that the Messiah—the Savior and Redeemer—has
already come to mankind, but they are expecting his appearance every moment. By no means do I want to shake your
personal faith in Jesus, David, but it is indeed a question of
faith. Jews do not believe that the Messiah has already fulfilled
his mission. Evil and injustice are still an integral part of our
world. Where is the promised paradise on Earth? Have bloody
wars ceased? Have people stopped tormenting and killing one
another in both small and large numbers? Have robberies, sufferings, and insults stopped since the coming of the one you
call the Messiah? Has mankind become more perfect, toler-
ant, and more compassionate in the last twenty centuries?"

David sat opposite me, frowned, and thought of a worthwhile answer.

"I really don't understand what you are talking about,
Vladimir!" he said resolutely. "Everyone knows that Jesus
Christ is the Messiah, who appeared on Earth and three days
after his crucifixion was resurrected and ascended into heaven.
Why are you shaking your head? It's as clear as day! You know
what? I will talk to the pastor of my church about it, and in a
week I'll prove to you that you are totally mistaken."

"Very well, David. Though I did not know you were planning to visit me in a week, I do not object at all. Come, and
let's have another talk," I said. "I ask only one thing: do not
think that I am trying to change your views on your faith.
Believe me, as a man who truly believes in God, you are
much closer to me spiritually than somebody who is an atheist. We just see some things in different ways. I also firmly
believe in the Messiah, but, unlike you, I do not believe that

he has already performed his mission on Earth. And who knows? There is a chance the Messiah will help us solve our dispute if he appears to people on Earth before we finish our conversation."

David did not hide his disappointment.

"I see what you mean, Vladimir," he said, his face gradually turning red. "But the problem is with you, not with me. It is you who are mistaken. I have nothing to do with it! I am only here to help you."

I could have said that I never asked my guest for help, but I decided not to.

In a few minutes, David had gained full control over his emotions.

"Okay. When I come to you next time, we'll discuss this issue more," he promised, "and now, before I leave, I will give you some very important and interesting literature that I have brought especially for you, my friend."

He opened his leather briefcase, took out a pile of brochures and solemnly presented them to me.

"Now you have something remarkable to occupy yourself with. When I come back, we will discuss in detail what you gleaned from this important literature. I will try to give you answers to any questions you might have."

Because I did not want to hurt David's feelings, I accepted the literature he offered and later looked through it. As might be expected, the main subject of the brochures was an appeal to readers to save their souls in order to be guaranteed a place in heaven. All that was required was to believe in the divine nature of Jesus and to become a regular visitor to the church at the address provided. With a sigh, I gathered the material neatly and put it away.

David returned as promised.

"Vladimir, you won't believe what a wonderful surprise is awaiting you today," he said with unconcealed enthusiasm before he even crossed the threshold of my apartment.

His face radiated optimism.

"Do you remember, Vladimir, last time you told me that since the Bible was prohibited in Russia you never had a chance to own it?"

David was right. During his previous visit, I mentioned to him that the Book of Books of the Jewish people, the Pentateuch, which spoke about the equality of all nations and appealed for love and sympathy for one's neighbors and peace on Earth, was assigned by the oppressive communist system to the category of seditious literature. The Communist Party was good at constantly praising itself for creating a paradise on Earth, but it never tolerated any opposition from competing ideologies and dealt harshly with anyone who questioned the Communist Party's ridiculous attempts to declare itself the beginning and end of everything in the world.

"So, now," continued David, "you have your own copy of the Bible, and guess what? It's in Russian, your native tongue. My pastor became very interested in your family when I told him about you. As soon as he finds time he will meet you all. Meanwhile he sent you this book as a present."

Unfortunately, the Bible David gave me was a Christian version. It consisted of two parts: the Hebrew Bible, which Christians call the Old Testament, and the New Testament.

Trying my best not to insult my guest, I expressed my appreciation for the gift but returned the book, explaining that, though I respect his views, I am only interested in the Hebrew Bible, and do not need the New Testament.

"Sorry, David. On our way to the United States, we spent six weeks in Rome. There, somebody gave me the Jewish Bible, so I do not need another copy."

"You are wrong to refuse, my friend. Why should you reject what you do not know?" David responded. "You should at least look through the New Testament. This holy book is read by millions of people, and you can find a lot of important things in it for yourself."

Once again, I expressed my appreciation for the present but insisted that I didn't want it.

"By the way, Vladimir," he said, "I hope you have really thought over our last conversation."

"Of course I thought it over," I answered, "but I hope that you did the same, and I hope I was able to convince you of the validity of my arguments."

David was clearly surprised. He sincerely did not expect anyone to question the truths he presented. Like many other Christian missionaries I met later, he thought that the monopoly on right and wrong belonged only to him.

"Are you joking, Vladimir?" he said, with a wide smile. "I took what you said last time as a big joke. How can you doubt the innumerable times Holy Scripture confirms the authenticity of the life, activity, and teachings of Jesus Christ, ours and your Savior and Redeemer? Everyone knows it, even a child! You better listen to what the prophet Isaiah says about it."

David began to recite by heart one of Isaiah's well-known quotes.

This was the first time I encountered what would become a recurring experience: Christian missionaries would cite extracts from Judaic sources to prove that, as far back as several hundred years before the birth of Jesus, the Biblical sages predicted his appearance.

From the Jewish point of view, these alleged prophecies were tailored through translation both semantically and grammatically to be predictions. And even with that, the listener needs to have a rich imagination.

Citing Biblical and Christian prophets, David, like many Christian missionaries, used a characteristic mechanical narration. Monotonously, not thinking about the content of the text, he narrated extracts by heart, mostly from the book of the prophet Isaiah, then of the prophets Jeremiah, Zachariah, and Daniel.

"You have an incredible memory," I complimented David, "and nobody could deny that you know the Bible very well. I am not able to quote the Bible by heart. But we are having a discussion now, and we live in a free country. You, as a native of this country, should know better than I do that I have the right to have my own views, just as you do. I have told you many times how much I respect your faith, and that is why I am not going to argue with you. You just have to understand that, as a Jew, I believe in the One God, who gave the Torah to the Jewish people, making a covenant with this people and making them His partners on Earth. Naturally, we will never agree on this point, but there are more things we agree on than there are differences between us, don't you think?"

"My friend, you react in a negative way simply because you have no idea how wonderful it is to be a Christian," David answered. "It's hard for me to describe it. You must see and experience it for yourself. We Christians, like one big family, help and care for each other. We'll talk about it more some other time, but now I want to tell you about another great offer, one you cannot turn down. Vladimir, I have a proposal for you, something that is really pleasant and useful for both our families. I know well the difficulties faced by new immigrants. So listen! Not far from here, my parents have a house that they usually rent, but at the moment it's empty. I talked to my wife and she agreed with my suggestion that our families could live there together. Our families would have different bedrooms, but we would share the other parts of this comfortable house. This way we'll have a small community of our own. I know at the moment you are short of money. You'll be able to save a lot because you won't have to pay rent.

"Just imagine," David spoke with enthusiasm, "our families will become close friends; we'll talk about religion and exchange languages. Your wife and son, as well as you, will benefit a lot by communicating with native English speakers. And don't forget that while we live together you'll be able to get acquainted with the American way of life. In addition to all that, our church is very close to our future house. It's a beautiful building, a real work of art. You'll like it. It'll be great! Our families will go to church together on Sundays! Very soon you'll understand all the beauty of Christianity! I don't remember if I told you that two families of former Soviet Jews already go to our church. You'll find it very interesting to talk to them. They are also doctors by profession. In short, a new world will open for you. Our pastor is a very educated, modern man. In our church, you'll feel right at home. So what do you say to that?"

It was too much for me.

"Excuse me, but I don't like it at all, David," I said firmly. "Let's begin from the fact that, at present, I'm too busy to introduce any new big changes into my life. I have just arrived in this country, and soon I must take exams to return to my profession. Besides, I have no desire to live in a commune of any type, even with your family. I had enough of that in the country I came from. And now, the most important thing: as far as I remember, I never mentioned to you anything about a desire to change my faith. Since you want to convert me to Christianity, let me remind you that I love my Jewish religion and am devoted to it as strongly as you love and are devoted to yours. To me, Judaism as a religion seems more natural, logical, and convincing. I was born a Jew, and I will die a Jew. For example, I cannot believe in the Holy Trinity, as it contradicts one of the main precepts of my monotheistic religion. While Jews have an unshakable faith in the singleness of God, Christians believe that the One is Three. One more disagreement between our religions is that, according to the Christian faith, Jesus was God and human at the same time. If he had been a man, then his death, though painful, horrible, merciless, and tragic, could not be connected with heaven. If he had been God, then he would not have experienced pain as we mortals do. And if he had been God, then he would not have been subject to the suffering that redeemed the human race from its sins. There is much more that could be said on this issue.

"For example, some Christians believe in the divine nature of the Holy Virgin and numerous saints, which further efface and dilute the concept of One God, a concept that is fundamental for a religion of monotheism as I understand it."

David, who was visiting me not to discuss but to present his point of view, did not at all like what I was saying. Now he was moving restlessly on the chair waiting for me to finish.

"Okay. Enough of that," he interrupted me.

"Just let me finish," I continued. "Since you were telling me about the beauty of your religion—and I fully understand the sincerity and good intentions of your words—all I want is to let you know that I consider my religion beautiful as well. And to parallel your position, I don't see why someone who became well acquainted with Judaism would not genuinely want to become a Jew. As a matter of fact, let's start with you, David. Why don't you at least consider converting to Judaism?"

As could be expected, David did not hesitate to voice a strong protest.

"How dare you offer this to me," he said angrily. "I will never convert to your faith, never in my life! What do I need your Judaism for? Don't you understand why I visit you and waste my precious time here?"

"Indeed, David, why do you come to me? We don't exchange our languages, and this visit, if I am not mistaken, was entirely your idea."

"Why don't you understand? I am coming to you for your own good. I follow one of the most important covenants of my church, which urges me to save the souls of unbelievers. I am already Christian, and you are not yet—so tell me, who needs to save his soul, you or me?"

"This sounds really strange, David! When you first came to me you said that you wanted us to exchange languages. You did not mention that, in reality, you wanted to convert me to your religion. So there was a misunderstanding, for which I am not going to blame you. Anything can happen. But since we are talking about conversion to another religion, and since we're on equal footing in this country, why is it not legitimate for me to offer you conversion to Judaism by the same token as you are trying to convert me to Christianity? You are a good man, David, and you could make an excellent Jew. Let's begin with your name; it is perfect for that undertaking."

Before I finished my phrase, without saying goodbye, my visitor quickly picked up his briefcase, threw the door open, ran out of my apartment, pressed the elevator button, jumped in, and disappeared from my life forever.

ALMOST A LINGUIST

SEVERAL MONTHS LATER, I passed the most important medical exam enabling the practice of medicine. Therefore, I had more free time, and I started searching for a pediatric residency or another job.

One evening, my wife asked me to pick up the phone. Some man wanted to speak to me. I said hello and asked him what I could do for him. Before answering my question, he—in impeccable Russian—asked in a pleasant, velvety-soft voice if it was true that my family had immigrated to this country recently.

"Good day," he continued, hearing my affirmative answer. "Welcome to the United States of America. I learned about you from Jewish Family Services. My name is Korney Voevodin. I am a pastor of a Baptist church. People call me Father Korney. My church is different from others, because besides ordinary matters, we actively maintain international contacts with religious organizations in the Soviet Union and Latin America. At present, due to the changes occurring in Soviet society, we are facing the necessity of modernizing the Russian language used in our religious literature. We want more people to understand the word of God. For that purpose, we are looking for educated people who have recently arrived from the U.S.S.R., like you and your wife, and who can speak contemporary Russian to help us. I do hope that you will find my offer interesting, especially because we would financially compensate you for the time you spend with us."

"It sounds tempting," I answered, "but it seems to me that we cannot really help you in that work. We are not specialists in languages, we are recent immigrants to this country, and we do not have a minute to spare. And what is most important, we are Jewish and not Christian."

"Let us begin from the end. It absolutely does not matter that you are not Christians; the only thing that interests us is your knowledge of the modern Russian language. As I just said, we are pragmatic people and understand very well that we might disturb your everyday life. That is why we offer you fair compensation for the time you spend on this assignment. I am sure you know better than I do how much religious life is neglected in Russia, so even your small but important contribution to the cause of getting the Bible through to a wider public will help those living behind the Iron Curtain to better understand God's words."

Eventually, Father Korney's arguments persuaded my wife and me to take part in the suggested project. Father Korney was glad to hear that we agreed; he informed me that the work on the religious literature would begin in a few weeks. But, for now, he invited us to visit him.

Since we—recent immigrants—hardly knew any Americans, we were pleased with Father Korney's invitation. We were interested and intrigued to meet and speak with native Russian speakers who had settled in America a long time before we did.

A week later, together with our son, after riding two city buses, we reached our destination at the appointed time. Father Korney lived in a small, comfortable house adjacent to his church on Kedzie Avenue. In addition to Father Korney and his wife, there were some of his relatives and three or four other married couples at the gathering. The welcome they gave us was more than hospitable. There was a lot of food on the table in the dining room; we, who were new people in the country, were either not able to afford many of those products and dishes, or didn't even know of their existence.

Before the meal, all the guests sitting at the table joined hands and, together with Father Korney uttered prayers. The conversation at the table was mostly about religious life in the Soviet Union and the persecution suffered by Christians there. I tried to say several times that Judaism was also suppressed by the state, but Father Korney and his guests, after politely listening to me, skillfully shifted the conversation to Christian subjects.

At parting, Father Korney and his wife expressed their delight in having met us and more than once said that they could not wait to start working on the modernization of the archaic text of the Bible.

"I admire your commitment to your religion," Father Korney told me with a gracious smile before we left, "but do not forget that Christianity has been the most popular religion in the world for two millennia."

"That's true," I answered, "but it is also a fact that in neither science nor religion is the truth established by a majority vote."

"Next time, we will discuss this subject in more detail," Father Korney promised cheerfully with a smile and then invited us to another family dinner.

We met a month later. As on the previous occasion, our host spoke the most. He talked about the methods used by Christians to allow religious organizations of the West to regularly provide many believers in the Soviet Union with educational materials despite strict censorship by the Soviet authorities.

During one of the pauses, I again reminded those present that in Russia religious Jews suffered no less severe persecution than Christians.

"Sure. We know about that," said Father Korney's wife. "But still, it is just a pity that the interests of Jews are confined only to the Old Testament. We believe the Bible makes no sense without the New Testament; the Old Testament is a kind of introduction to the new one."

"On the other hand," I objected, "it's a pity that so few Christians have read our Torah, or as you call it, the Old Testament, because the New Testament constantly refers to the Hebrew Bible. Without the Old Testament, there would be no New Testament."

There was no response.

Before we left, Father Korney told us that work on the project would start very soon.

"I am sure that you will find this work very interesting," he said. "And I want to mention once more that you will be offered a fair compensation for your time."

Three weeks later, we visited Father Korney again. This time we met in the church. Entering the room where we were to start work on the project, my wife Marina and I were surprised to find that there were other couples there.

Looking more closely at them, I noticed that these people, like us, were recent Soviet Jewish immigrants. We had met many of them before at immigration organizations in Vienna and Rome and, by that time, in Chicago as well.

As usual, Father Korney's church was generous. Near one of the walls of the meeting room, there was a table with lots of food. When we arrived, the audition of the candidates for the project of modernizing the Bible was in full swing. While each couple demonstrated their linguistic skills in Father Korney's study, in the meeting room there was a solemn silence.

The event was organized in an exemplary manner. We had hardly come into the meeting room when one of the church volunteers approached us, offering to take care of our son while we were busy. Having received our consent, she took him to a playroom, where he joined other children.

After a short wait, it was our turn to demonstrate our linguistic skills. Two assistants—a man and a woman—were sitting on either side of Father Korney. First, the man read a passage from the Biblical text, and then we, in turns, offered our rendering of the archaic text into modern Russian. Our examiners nodded their heads approvingly while they listened to our revised versions, carefully writing them down in their notebooks. Prior to this event, neither my wife nor I had suspected we had a talent for translation, but judging by the excited faces of our examiners, one would think that they had found in us the prospective leading authors of the revised version of the Bible.

Alas, our pride at these previously unsuspected linguistic talents did not last long. To our surprise, when we returned to the waiting room and joined the other candidates, whose Russian, as we knew from our previous contact, was very far from perfect, we learned that the "examination board" told each member of the group that they all, without exception, had outstanding literary talents as well.

When all the candidates had been given an audition, Father Korney, accompanied by his assistants, joined the Jewish audience—the future revisers of Christian texts in Russian.

They started serving coffee and tea. A more serious treat awaited us "literature experts" at the end of the meeting.

At a signal from Father Korney, one of his assistants pressed a button and a movie screen slowly descended from the ceiling. The light was turned off and a film began. Oddly enough, the theme of the movie was not in any way associated with the translation activity. The film was about the world's Christian movement and lasted for about thirty minutes; its general message was that Christianity is the embodiment of the absolute truth and that only faith in Jesus can give a sense of purpose to human life by granting real happiness and eternal life in heaven. The next film was a documentary about the life and times of St. Peter.

I gradually realized that the real reason for holding this event was not the examination of linguistic skills of the invited audience but the promotion of Christianity.

Honestly speaking, I felt really sorry for Father Korney. He had such a bright mind, nice character, hospitality, a noble profession, and an impressive appearance, and he had used all those attributes to employ a rather primitive method of luring an unsuspecting audience into a trap to sell his religion.

What happened later proved my theory. When the film finished and the light was turned on, Father Korney, with a paternal smile, addressed the audience, asking what we thought about the presented material.

There was a long pause. People were smiling uneasily, but nobody wanted to speak out. Then Father Korney began to review the films himself.

"The true Christian faith," he said in a solemn tone of voice, "is the only guarantee of purging a human soul of past, present, and future sins. Only through this faith do believers have the precious opportunity to communicate with Jesus Christ and save their sinful souls from eternal damnation."

"Ladies and gentlemen," he summed up, "how can a reasonable person reject such a priceless reward as eternal life in heaven? And all that is necessary to obtain this gift is just a small step. That's all."

Before the fifteen-minute break, beautifully printed reading materials with glossy covers and calendars of the Baptist movement were handed out to the audience. Then we were informed that in the next part of the meeting a family from Kiev, who recently converted to Christianity, would speak to us and that their presentation would be followed by a musical program.

Thus, instead of modernizing the archaic language of the Bible, as planned, we now had to spend another hour or two of our precious time on useless and uncalled-for propaganda.

Marina and I decided that it was time to leave. We had no desire to cease to be Jewish. I started to pack up our things while my wife went to get our son.

Our compatriots were still sitting, talking quietly among themselves.

"Tell me, Lyubochka, how many times I told you, my dear, that I like Christianity, but you never listen to me," a middle-aged man who had recently arrived from Moscow was telling his wife, who gave him a nod of approval as she painted her lips bright red while carefully gazing at her reflection in a portable, round mirror.

"Now you can learn how incredibly interesting this religion is. And let me tell you one more thing. Pasternak and Brodsky, both great poets, would not have turned to Christianity if they had not found it worthwhile. I am glad that we were invited here, especially because they will treat us to a superb dessert, which, of course, you like more than anything."

"Why are you leaving?" My countryman from Odessa and an acquaintance from Rome, who had a Semitic appearance similar to Lyubochka's husband, turned to me. "Believe me, I am not interested in religion at all. One could even say I'm an atheist. So what does it matter to me, or to you, what they say to us. Christianity, Islam, Buddhism—what difference does it make to us? Let it go in one ear and out the other. I look at all this activity the same way as we did back in the Soviet Union: they talk, we listen. They have their agenda, we have ours. At least stay here until they give us money, which we honestly deserve for the time spent. Do you think anyone would be sitting here if they were not going to pay us? But remember when we met back in Italy? Don't you think it's true that Christians have reached perfection in architecture and painting? During our Italian holidays on the way from Russia to the US, my wife and I visited maybe all the churches in Rome. What architecture! What interiors! And the Vatican—how beautiful it is! Honestly, if anti-Semites would stop reminding me that I am Jewish, I would probably take much more interest in Christianity."

At that time, I did not yet know that for some Christians converting people—and especially "the stiff-necked Jews"—to

Christianity is considered the fulfillment of an important religious duty allegedly prescribed by Jesus himself.

Every time another Jew changes his religion, irreparable damage is done to the whole Jewish people. After centuries of a history full of tragic events, Jews, without hesitation, preferred to die a painful death rather than convert to another religion. For them, the organic and inseparable connection with God was not an illusory reality or an empty formality, but the tangible and salutary essence of their lives. This attitude toward religion was dominant among the majority of Jews in the quite recent past and continues to be such for most of our people. And now, in our own time, a few smooth phrases, uttered with cheap aplomb by a self-confident preacher, are enough for some people with supposedly critical minds to embrace a new religion. These people easily forget that only recently they lived in an environment where for hundreds of years unbridled anti-Semitism, humiliating their human dignity, was maintained and supported by generations of preachers of Orthodox Christianity. Is it not a bit surprising that, in this country, where everyone can make an independent, free choice, some Jews, by rejecting the religion of their fathers, use this freedom to thoughtlessly deny the proud history of many preceding generations of their people?

The Soviet Jews had a healthy, cynical attitude toward the official propaganda spread by the Soviet government, justly considering it brainwashing. It is difficult to believe that, after such extensive life experience, these worldly people with a good deal of healthy skepticism let themselves be persuaded by all kinds of propaganda.

WHAT MAKES
A JEW "JEWISH"

BEFORE OUR ENTRANCE to America, during interviews with the US Ambassador, my fellow countrymen—future citizens of the United States—claimed refugee status in a sincere manner on the basis that we, the Soviet Jews, were not allowed to freely practice our religion in the Soviet Union. This was the decisive argument that convinced the representative of the American government to grant Soviet Jews refugee status—a status most desirable for new immigrants. However, now that we have entered the United States, and our dream to live in the country where everyone is free to join any synagogue has become reality, some Jews—forgetting their complaint about the lack of freedom to practice Judaism—do not seek spiritual satisfaction in the religion of their ancestors but in other places.

It is really surprising to observe the approach to religion by former citizens of an atheist state. Dealing with my compatriots who currently live in the US, Israel, and Germany, I have received plenty of evidence that, despite their negative attitude to Soviet propaganda, many of them did inherit from it what had been drummed into their heads since childhood; namely, the contemptuous, suspicious, and often hostile views on religion.

What makes a Jew Jewish? Is it belonging to the same race, genealogy, language, culture, set of ideas, or residence in the same geographic location? The answer is no, none of those factors. There are Jews who have different skin colors and different appearances, who belong to different social groups and speak different languages. They live in many countries of the world, are imbued with elements of different world cultures, and often cannot be distinguished from the rest of the local population. The only common denominator identifying and bringing together all generations of Jews has always been our eternal monotheistic religion, our faith in one God, whose voice sounds clearly and expressively from the pages of the Torah. Modern Jews visiting many traditional synagogues in different parts of the world appeal to God with the same prayers, listen to the same melodies that our ancestors used to address God for many centuries. At the same time of the day (adjusted to different time zones), Jews throughout the world appeal to God with identical prayers. They observe the same rituals some dating back to the time before the temples were destroyed in Jerusalem.

From a bird's-eye view, one can observe Jews throughout the whole world at the same hour and minute lighting Shabbat and festival candles, singing the same religious songs, baking matzo on Passover, building *sukkahs* and gathering at rivers and reservoirs on the first day of the Jewish New Year to perform the *Tashlich* ceremony, symbolizing cleansing of one's sins. A devoted faith in the word of the Torah has been the eternal torch that Jews have successfully and proudly carried with them through many centuries until the present. That is why it is logical to suppose that Jews who seek answers to burning spiritual questions would not be motivated to find them in the religions they know only by hearsay, nor in the religions which have humiliated and insulted them for many centuries, but within their own hospitable, eternal, and fruitful religion.

It is only when a joyous event happens in the family—such as a wedding, the birth of a child, a B'nai Mitzvah ceremony—or a tragic one—such as the sickness or death of a dear one—that many Jews who had been trying their best to avoid conversations about God and religion, for a short time recover from their deep hibernation and remember the existence of their eternal human spirit. When this happens, these awakened people—willingly professing their faith in God—forget that only yesterday they carelessly brushed Him aside and, at best, smiled skeptically when others reminded them of His existence. But if we recognize the existence of God in special moments of our lives, what prevents us from doing it every day? Why don't we address Him with words of appreciation and respect, at least, for the truly miraculous chance and opportunity to live and think among the free people that inhabit the only hospitable blue planet known to us in the huge infinite space of the universe?

Shouldn't those who express their belief in merciful God be thankful to Him for giving them their precious, healthy grandchildren, parents, a home, bread, and a profession? Is it not a miracle that in many countries of the world each of us can enter any synagogue with heads held high and shake hands with other representatives of our ancient and eternal people who run a millennial relay race to hand us the baton of our unblemished faith? Should we not be thankful to the creator for endowing us with wonderfully tuned and self-regulating bodies and immortal spirits that vibrate in unison with the pulse of God's presence?

In everyone's life there are bitter and tragic moments, but even then there is always something very significant for which a believer wants to offer praise to the creator.

This testimony of devotion is convincingly illustrated by the centuries-old history of our people. Generation after generation of Jews went to trial and death with a prayer addressed to their God on their lips. Jews passionately prayed to God, individually and collectively, during numerous persecutions and pogroms, and even during the recent monstrous crime against humanity—the Holocaust. Through our long history our people have been faithful to our great religion, and it was not by chance that Judaism became the basis for two other great monotheistic religions—Christianity and Islam—preceding them by millennia.

It is difficult to accept the fact that representatives of our ancient religious tradition forget that they are a part of collective history. It is surprising and painful to see how some Jews easily and willingly reject their unique heroic past—a past that was praised by poets and writers of many nations—and how they allow illiterate missionaries, who juggle a dozen phrases learned by rote, to convince them of the pseudo truths that are so far from the genuine historical essence of our heritage. What kind of revelation do the gullible listeners expect to hear from yet another missionary who, in a robot-like manner, mutters under his breath quotes from the Torah or the prophets taken arbitrarily out of context? Why should those Jews seek to encounter eternity and God in the foreign home of Christianity or other religions when their own personal origin presents them with the gift of a unique opportunity to be an indelible part of the religion of Abraham, Isaac, and Jacob? A minimal knowledge of Judaism is enough to put in his place a missionary who mumbles sheer nonsense while trying to convince his listeners of absurd truths.

Next time you become a subject for brainwashing by missionaries who approach you on the street with smiles, or come knocking at your door to tell you about the promises of their religion, greet them politely, but before they start their propaganda, let them know why you think Judaism is a great religion and why it is the religion of your choice. The knowledge of most missionaries is confined to mechanically memorized material and is usually devoid of deep knowledge. They are taught and prepared to act as initiators of verbal persuasion, and they become helpless if they have to defend their own opinions. The most self-assured among them can be discouraged from continuing to deliver the propaganda they build on sand with a few minutes of educated opposition to their ideas.

"Good morning," I greet another preacher, who knocks at my door uninvited or stops me on the street. "It is really nice to meet you. Thank you for your concern, but since you desire to talk about your religion, would you first let me tell you about the beauty and truth of my Jewish religion? Perhaps after our conversation you might decide to consider Judaism."

Such an approach always works: practically one hundred percent of missionaries, who, with the best intentions, sincerely wish to change my faith, leave me alone and never come back. It is even easier to ignore the street preachers. In our free country, no one can make another person listen to missionaries' appeals and claims that *they* have the key to the absolute truth.

THE INEXTRICABLE LINK
BETWEEN GENERATIONS

DESPITE THE GREAT CONTRIBUTIONS that Jews have
made to world science and culture, they still remain one of the
smallest nations. So, proportionally, when only one Jew rejects
the religion of his fathers, it is equivalent to thousands of
Christians changing their faith. That's why it is so difficult for
Jews to be dispassionate when our fellow Jews put crosses on
their necks in an ostentatious manner. According to Judaism,
anybody born to a Jewish mother remains a Jew, despite any
attempts to reject his or her religious heritage. Therefore,
Jews can escape from their families, leave their country, but
they cannot get away from themselves without the risk of
living a double life. Countless examples prove that, in the
eyes of non-Jews, a convert to Christianity is not regarded
as a real Christian, but as an alien, as "a Jew who decided to
accept Christianity."

In 1954, three months before I turned thirteen, my uncle
Semyon, my father's elder brother, visited us. That was the
first and last time I ever met him. Before the war, he was a
secretary of the Dnepropetrovsk regional committee of the
Party. A short time before Germany occupied Poland, he was
authorized to have an official meeting with Polish Jewish

communists who—facing the impending danger of approaching fascism—had escaped to Russia. For nothing else but the sheer fact of that meeting, Uncle Semyon was accused of Trotskyism and was imprisoned for thirteen years.

Released via amnesty after Stalin's death in 1953, he was among the first who were freed. Uncle Semyon's faithful Ukrainian wife, who had been patiently waiting for him all that time, and his fifteen-year-old son Gregory, who, according to his papers, was not a Jew but a Ukrainian, were happy to see him back. After Uncle Semyon's release from prison they settled in Benderi, a Moldovan town, where, because of his previous organizational skills, my uncle was appointed the head of a local brewery.

Looking ahead, it should be mentioned that happy family life did not last long for him: two years after his release, Uncle Semyon died of tuberculosis, which he had contracted in the early years of his prison sentence.

A thirteen-year stay in prison could not shake my uncle's faith in fairness and the final victory of the communist experiment. From his conversations with my father, I understood that he believed he had been convicted by mistake, by the commonly accepted principle, "You cannot make an omelet without breaking eggs," but that Stalin and the regime itself deserved the deepest respect. Despite my young age, I could not help but wonder why the years of serving his long sentence did not make my uncle less faithful to the idea of communism.

After such a long separation my father discussed a lot of different subjects with his brother. I learned Uncle Semyon's plan for my future when my father, with an air of mystery, invited me into another room to talk.

I took a seat on a backless chair they offered me, while my uncle, periodically coughing into his handkerchief and checking it for blood, stared at me from under his thick brows.

"Vovka," my father said, "I have to share one very important secret with you."

"Listen," he continued in an uncharacteristic, theatrical, and solemn voice, obviously wanting to persuade himself about what he was going to tell me. "I must tell you that, even though on your birth certificate it is written that I am your father, in reality, well, I'm not your father."

Completely unprepared for such shocking news, which in one moment deprived me of my parent and a part of my own self as well, I shivered with agitation. I felt as if the ground was slipping from under my feet and a bottomless abyss was opening up before me. Paralyzed, I was unable to say anything.

"Look how pale he's turned. Don't you worry, Vovka!" Uncle Semyon began to cheer me up. "Just listen carefully to what your father is telling you. We both wish you the best, and we are talking about your future."

"But I have no other dad but you," turning to my father, and getting indignant, I interrupted my uncle. "No one else can be my father but you!"

"Calm down," my father answered, conspiratorially winking at me. "The main thing is that whoever would be written up as your father would be Russian by nationality, and, consequently, you will be Russian too. Do you understand?"

"Never in my life would I agree to that," I cried.

"Come on, pull yourself together! Don't be afraid, as long as I am alive you'll be my son. Did not you yourself tell me many times how much you are upset with the insults you hear directed toward Jews? Remember my son, anti-Semitism has existed from time immemorial, and it will not disappear in the foreseeable future. Why should you be among those who are treated as if they are responsible for all human sins and therefore suffer injustice all your life? You don't even know how difficult it will be for you to enter any university and get a good education because you are Jewish. What difference does it make to you what is written on your papers? The main thing is to get higher education and then to become independent and free! And all that is required of you is just to come with your mother and me to a notary public office, where they will change your birth certificate. The rest I take upon myself."

My father's words did not convince me at all. My whole nature protested against the idea of making me someone I was not. I could not have another father except the one who was sitting beside me, the one whom I had been waiting impatiently for four years and six months to come back from war, and the one to whom I could always turn for help for protection from the world's misfortunes. There could be many fathers in the world, both good and bad, but only my own father and no one else was *my* father. Not for all the gold in the world, not for the chance to be an emperor's son, not, as was just suggested to me, the opportunity to become a representative of Russia or any other nation, would I change the desire to remain myself – myself and nobody else.

Being a Jew in the environment where I grew up promised many inconveniences in the future, but, since I had been born a Jew, that was my destiny and it was my duty, first of all, to learn how to live a full-fledged and happy life and secondly, to train myself not to pay attention to the prejudicial views of anti-Semites. Pretending to be someone else would be betraying my own self.

"Stop arguing and do whatever your father tells you to do, Vovka," Uncle Semyon said to me. "Take my family for example. Although I am Jewish, my son is Ukrainian like his mother, and everyone is happy about it. It will be much easier for him to enter university and make a career, and later to hold a good position. This also will allow him to go abroad. Plus, my son, Gregory Chromtchenko, does not need to hear insults from all kinds of idiots about his nationality. I don't understand at all what you are worried about. All you need to do is to be silent and not discuss this subject with anyone."

I refused to be persuaded.

"First of all, I do not need any other fathers but you," I said to my father. "Second, I want to be the person I was born to be. I don't want to live a double life. They could write in my birth certificate a hundred times that I am not a Jew; I will still feel that I am Jewish. Maybe some people can lie to themselves and to others that they are not who they are. I will never be able to do that. That's how I am."

The brothers exchanged glances.

"There is nothing to be done with him, Abrasha," my uncle said. "Your son is too young; he does not have enough wisdom to understand a simple truth. It's a pity, Vovka, that when you are old enough to make the right decision, it will be too late. Beware! You might regret it afterwards."

The brothers left me alone. My flat refusal to follow their plan left a strong impression, and my father never again raised the question of changing my nationality.

Now, many years after my father's unsuccessful attempt to turn me into a Russian, I think that if I, then a teenager with an immature personality, could not bear the thought of losing my identity, then how must an adult with a mature, established personality feel, pretending to be who he is not?

WELCOME TO
THE SYNAGOGUE

THE FIRST YEARS of our life in Chicago, like the first years for other immigrants, were filled with all kinds of problems connected with adapting to the new life. For me, the first objective was to return to pediatrics, the profession I had practiced for ten years before my arrival in America.

During this stressful period, neither my wife, Marina, nor I had time for more than episodic visits to a synagogue. Then a resident in pediatrics, I had to spend most of my time working long hours at the hospital, while my wife, besides having a job for which she was paid a minimum wage, was busy helping our son adjust to the new environment and taking care of the house.

In spite of our limited financial means, we were a happy family: our main dream to come to the West had come true, and now we were able to send our son to a Jewish religious school. At first this school lent us a helping hand—we were allowed to pay only half of the tuition.

There is nothing better for a Jewish child than a good, serious Jewish education. Thanks to such an education, our son became familiar with the Jewish religion, history, and culture and understood that he could be proud to belong to the Jewish nation. Since in the city children do not live close to

each other and rarely play unattended outside, we drove our
son to his school friends' homes, and his friends' parents, in
turn, brought their children to us.

The decision to send our son to a Jewish school played an
important role in the formation of his personality, but, not less
important, it also helped us, his parents, to assert ourselves in
the religious life of America.

My wife, who, despite her busy schedule, still had much
more free time than I, made an important discovery: attending a Saturday—Shabbat—service at the synagogue affiliated
with our son's school could be a source of deep spiritual pleasure. In time, thanks to her initiative and activity, we started to
celebrate Shabbat and major Jewish religious holidays at home.

At first, without previous preparation and knowledge of
the structure of the religious service or of Hebrew, we found
attendance at synagogue services to be quite difficult. It was
not easy to sit still when we had no idea what they were talking about. But we decided not to rush things, as we were sure
that with time we would accumulate enough knowledge, and
everything would fall into its rightful place. We did not hide
our ignorance of religion or shy from asking questions, and
there were always people ready to help us. We knew that we
were on the right track.

Although in the United States information is free and
unrestricted, a great number of American Jews whom we met
in Chicago had no idea of the pressure Jewish religious and
secular life had been under in the Soviet Union. They shook
their heads doubtfully when we told them that before we came
to this country we had no idea about keeping Shabbat, had
never been able to hear the Torah being read, knew practically

nothing about Jewish religious ceremonies and what most Jewish holidays signified.

The famous Yiddish writer Sholom Aleichem wrote a hundred years ago that in America everyone is in a hurry. Even in our synagogue, which by now we have visited for many years, our acquaintances have never shown real interest in the life of Jews in the U.S.S.R. At first, when they asked us the same questions like "Where did you come from?" "Whom did you leave in Russia?" or "Did they turn down your application at first?" I felt flattered, because they seemed to take an interest in what I was eager to tell them in detail. However, every time I began to describe about real life in Russia, my listeners in a very short time became distracted. It was not because people did not like what I was telling them, they just had many other things on their minds, so they were satisfied with a minimum of information, or, very possibly, they just wanted to show their interest. That's life.

People who only occasionally visit a synagogue often complain that "no one cares" about them. Most frequently, the reason for this alleged lack of interest from congregants is the respectful attitude of Americans towards the privacy of individuals and the lack of desire to interfere in other people's lives.

The time when a Jew would enter an unknown synagogue and everybody would ask him who he was, where he was from, whether he was married, whether he had children, was left behind in the Old World and will never come back. In our "enlightened" time, it is considered rude to interfere in other people's private lives with personal questions, and such interference is not welcomed by vocal advocates of political correctness.

Considering this, next time you visit a synagogue, do not think that people there don't care about you. They just do not want you to think that they are imposing.

And remember, "the squeaky wheel gets the oil." If you directly tell the regular visitors or a rabbi of a synagogue that you need help, you are sure to get it. People will be glad to answer your questions, for the simple reason that most people are eager to share their knowledge.

The process of learning about Judaism is impossible without the help of books and consultations with competent people. The material that might help you gain insight into Judaism is vast: apart from the written Torah known to most Jews, there are also oral laws or the oral Torah, books of prophets, and the Talmud, with its innumerable commentaries and an ocean of books on Jewish theology.

THE ETERNAL PEOPLE

WHILE GERMAN FASCISM wanted to annihilate Jews first ideologically and then physically, the Soviet Union never abandoned the hope of destroying the Jewish people spiritually by dissolving them and gradually assimilating them into Soviet culture.

Vladimir Lenin certainly defended Jews in some of his works, but always on the premise that they would forget their historical identity, their ancient religion, and their rich culture.

Consistently implementing Lenin's and later Stalin's vision for Jewish people, the Communist Party did not take into consideration the resilience of the undying Jewish people. Centuries-old history of the children of Israel proved their adaptability, and flexibility. Over three hundred years ago, King Louis XIV of France asked Blaise Pascal, the great Christian philosopher, to give him proof of God's existence. Pascal answered, "Why the Jews, your Majesty, the Jews!"

Nowadays, when the "millennial" fascist empires are in ruins, the Jewish people, despite the catastrophe inflicted on them by those who wanted to annihilate them, continue their confident march through the pages of human history. The Torah serves them as a reliable compass.

From the time of the Diaspora, Jews in different parts of the world were diverse in culture, language, and outward appearance. However, historically, the vast majority of Jews in the world were united by their selfless faith in the One God, the God of Abraham, Isaac, and Jacob, the God who, through His divine revelation, gave His covenant to Moses on Mount Sinai.

Thanks to strength and confidence in the rightness of their faith, our people have endured countless tyrants and despots, preserving up to the present the purity of our religion. Sharing their talents with other nations fairly and enthusiastically, the Jewish people will never forget that the Torah, the Talmud, and works by innumerable Jewish scholars present their most precious spiritual heritage.

Those modern Jews who, for various reasons, are doing their best to distance themselves from their religion should not forget that Judaism, from ancient times to this day, has had a great influence on Western culture. Songs in Yiddish which many non-religious Jews like to sing were created in an environment where faith in God went without saying, where children from an early age went to *cheder*, where Jewish marriages were a rule, where people died with the name of God on their lips.

The history of our people abounds with stories of heroic acts. The inspiration for numerous Jewish heroes to perform great deeds was frequently prompted by their faith in the God of Israel and the ethical principles of the Torah.

Jews believe that nothing has a more elevated purpose than a life dedicated to the noble actions inspired by the word of God expressed on the pages of the Torah and the writings of the prophets. For that reason, faithful Jews, trying to be worthy partners of God on Earth, devote their lives to the cause of peace and prosperity, and to partnership with God in making this world better. The famous historian Paul Johnson writes in his book, *A History of the Jews*, that the world owes to the Jewish people such great ideas as the equality of all before God and under human laws; individual conscience and redemption; the concept of peace where peace is considered a concrete—not an abstract—ideal; love as a basis for justice; and many other concepts which today constitute the moral principles of the modern human worldview.

JEWISH RELIGIOUS
WEEKDAYS AND HOLIDAYS

REGULAR WORSHIP SERVICES, especially in an orthodox synagogue, are remarkable for the active involvement of those who participate in them. On their first visit to a synagogue, people find many things strange or difficult to understand. Certainly, it is hard for uninitiated newcomers to discern the structure and direction of the religious service.

When we started attending the synagogue, we had a similar experience. But when we gained a better insight into what was happening, we realized how logical and straightforward the structure of worship was. A serious and patient attitude toward what was happening in the synagogue during the prayers proved to be enough for us to actively participate in the religious service. It is sufficient to know the fundamentals of the Jewish religion and to initiate the process that ultimately makes the synagogue a second home, a desirable place to offer up prayers and conversation with God among fellow Jews and well-wishers.

One reason Judaism attracts people who think critically, who actively seek God, is that our religion does not prohibit or evade discussions of the difficult questions in the Torah, those that appear controversial and confusing at first. Judaism has always welcomed discussion and resolution of what sometimes appear to be challenges to common sense.

Since Jewish religious teaching covers a vast array of historical, ethical, and psychological aspects, there is boundless material for study—truly an ocean. The Talmud and numerous books by Jewish sages and teachers are often intentionally dedicated to a discussion of things that a novice in religion may find surprising, either for their seeming naïveté or their incomprehensibility from the viewpoint of modern ethical principles. Less difficult questions can be resolved with a little help, while more controversial issues from the Torah and the Talmud, which might confuse an inexperienced reader, can be addressed in different ways, for example, by comparing and examining many corresponding comments accumulated through the long history of Judaism and offered by the best rabbinical minds. In cases where the wise men and teachers of Judaism themselves are unable to reach an explanation or understanding of some particular hard-to-understand question, they frankly admit this and say openly that the solution of that controversial issue will only be possible after the coming of the Messiah.

The study of religion should be made without prejudices, without distraction by personal or minor issues, and without preconceived notions about concepts that at first appear to contradict the moral and ethical principles of the non-religious observer. Imperative to such study is a strong belief in the existence of God of the universe, who created this world, who gave life to all living things, and who set before mankind countless questions filled with impenetrable mystery.

The impenetrable mystery of human existence will always intrigue those who try to fathom the bottomless depths of

God's revelation. Just like the materialists who themselves never stopped in their resolute drive to unravel natural phenomena, those who search for God should never be discouraged by external difficulties.

In addition to the knowledge of the structure of worship, it is interesting and instructive to study the essence and contents of the religious ceremonies performed during Shabbat and the main Jewish High Holy Days—Rosh Hashanah and Yom Kippur—and such festivals as Passover, Purim, Sukkot, Shavuot, and Hanukkah. Such information can be gleaned from widely available literature, and from conversations with rabbis and knowledgeable people.

In America—the country of freedom—nobody imposes religious views on others, and anyone who wishes to get any kind of religious education can enjoy limitless opportunities to do so. But in order to gain insight into the basics of religion, a person must apply his or her own initiative.

Even a superficial knowledge of the Torah allows the reader to perceive the greatness of its text. Compared to eternity, human life is too short, and, much as we may want to read all the books we find interesting, it is impossible even to look through most of them. In order to attain the quintessence of available knowledge during one's lifetime, one needs to choose the most important, the most essential texts to read. In our civilization, such an important and necessary book—the most popular book for millions of readers over many centuries—has always been and will always remain the Torah, which makes it possible for its readers to see their place in the universe. A careful study of the Torah, particularly in Hebrew, its original language, has inspired countless generations of Jews.

Our Torah tells us that all mankind originated from one married couple—Adam and Eve—and, consequently, the whole human race is nothing more than one big family whose members are equal and deserve equal respect.

Drafted under the undoubted influence of the teachings of the Torah, the American Declaration of Independence puts it thus: "We hold these truths to be self-evident, that all men are created equal, that they are endowed by their creator with certain unalienable Rights, that among these are Life, Liberty and the pursuit of Happiness." The principles of the Torah are also manifested in Article 55 of the UN Charter, which calls for universal respect for and observance of human rights and fundamental freedoms for all, regardless of their race, sex, language, or religion.

A monumental panorama chronicling Jewish life thousands of years ago unfolds on the pages of the five books of Moses, providing details of the history of the Jewish people and other nations beginning from the moment of creation.

The characters of the Torah exhibit the same feelings and passions as modern people and, despite its four-thousand-year history, the text and contents of the Jewish part of the Bible, which the Christians undeservedly call the *Old* Testament, is as relevant as if it had been written today. Nothing will ever be able to turn it into an *old* and somehow obsolete document. The message of the Torah is as relevant now as when it was given by God to Moses on Mount Sinai.

Apart from its original religious content, the Jewish Bible or TaNaKh [an acronym of the words: Torah, Neviim (Prophets), and Ktuvim (Scripts)] introduces readers to the wisdom of ancient men and familiarizes them with unprecedented poetic and literary works.

The text of the Bible becomes more comprehensible to a modern reader when viewed not as a list of dry events and descriptions, but as a text appealing to human hearts, which is aimed—often symbolically and allegorically—at the perception of the divine essence of reality and the everyday world.

For millennia, the unsurpassed text of the Pentateuch has served as an inexhaustible source of inspiration for artists, composers, and poets. Gaining more in-depth knowledge about the works of great ancient and medieval poets inspired by the Bible is in itself a good reason to study the Hebrew language.

Many generations of distinguished people have dedicated their lives to correlating the contents of the Torah with universal concepts of humanism and ethics.

During its long history, the Jewish religious tradition has accumulated an endless number of precious works that interest people with diverse tastes and demands. Among these works, one may find a whole gallery of masterpieces of human thought.

A person immersed in the study of the Bible and its commentaries lives in a world of exciting dialogues between people who, despite living in different epochs and places, were able to consecutively develop and advance a whole gamut of ideas connected by the Biblical narrative.

The doctrine of Jews being the chosen people is one example of something that at first seems incomprehensible and unpleasant to people brought up in the spirit of equality. But there are no grounds for such concern. Upon close analysis, this doctrine becomes much more logical and acceptable. The fact that they are chosen does not mean that Jews consider themselves better than other peoples. The Jews do not think they are in any way privileged in the sense of being entitled to special rewards; all they believe is that, initially, God offered the Torah to many nations, but only the Jews agreed to accept it with all its demands of observing six hundred and thirteen positive and negative commandments—the *Mitzvot*. Thus, having voluntarily accepted the Torah from God, Jews assumed an important mission they cannot avoid: to be, as a nation, a spiritual partner of God on earth. From this perspective, the concept of being the chosen nation is interpreted not as a privilege but as a yoke of responsibility to dedicate their entire lives to carrying out the numerous obligations of God's commandments.

Herman Branover, a world-famous physicist and Jewish educator, wrote in his still popular book, *Return*:

> "The Holy Torah and its commandments are the sole vessel capable of providing, in spite and in defiance of the natural order of things, a direct link between the Jewish people and God. The commandments are God's will clothed in a form intelligible to man. They constitute the outer skin, the attire by donning which man communicates with God. The Torah is God's sublime wisdom, the only source of knowledge available to man, whose mind, by embracing this wisdom, comes in direct contact with God, drawing light and life from higher realms, and rechanneling them to enrich our entire world."

When the prophet Isaiah exclaims in his sermons that Judaism should serve as a light for mankind, it means that Jews have to do their best to constantly study the Torah and the Talmud, observe the prescribed rituals, keep dietary laws, respect the Day of Eternity, Shabbat, and other Jewish religious holidays, and set for other nations a good example of faithful observance of God's commandments. For a sincere believer, observance of the prescribed rules is not a burden, but a special privilege that can bring him or her closer to the divine essence.

Following the established traditions of previous centuries, the best answer to the catastrophe that tragically befell our people during the Second World War must be the visible proof that our people are not broken, that we are alive and well, that our nation has not lost courage but continues to live and prosper and, moreover, has achieved a real miracle: reviving the Jewish state, Israel, in its historical homeland.

The well-known Jewish theologian Emil Fackenheim offered to add to the six hundred thirteen *Mitzvot* one more, the six hundred and fourteenth: Jews have no moral right to forget Jewish faith, not least of all because they should not hand Hitler a posthumous victory over the Jewish people.

THE SYNAGOGUE LIFE

My mother died in 1984. According to the Jewish tradition, children must recite *Kaddish*—the prayer for the dead—for a deceased parent over the following eleven months. In Orthodox synagogues, Kaddish is read in the presence of *minyan*, a group of ten or more Jewish men (in the Conservative and Reform synagogues both men and women are counted).

In order to read Kaddish for my mother, I started going to synagogue every morning.

Through daily attendance at religious services, I learned the great importance of collective prayer in Jewish religious life. In the presence of a minyan, on any day of the week, a Jew can join in communal prayer, praising and thanking God and appealing to Him for different needs, and can participate in the most important Jewish ceremonies.

At the end of eleven months of reading Kaddish, I suddenly realized that the minyan had become a part of my life. For years, when I woke in the morning, I had always felt a spiritual emptiness that I did not know how to deal with. My regular attendance at synagogue freed me from that irrational feeling once and for all. Obviously, discovering the world of religious meditation satisfied my inherent inner spiritual needs.

Morning prayers do not usually last long. In many synagogues, after the religious service is over, participants of the minyan are offered a small meal: coffee, tea, bagels, cream cheese. Daily minyan can be perceived as an extended family; its regular and not-so-regular participants like to celebrate birthdays and anniversaries, and commemorate those dear ones who have passed away by offering treats to fellow congregants at the end of the worship.

Newcomers to synagogues might feel a natural embarrassment at finding themselves in an unfamiliar situation, hearing an unfamiliar language, following unfamiliar rituals.

But none of it is rocket science. The temporary difficulties encountered in adapting to the new environment can easily be overcome. All that is necessary is desire and a little patience.

Becoming part of the synagogue's life is easy and natural. Mastering the elements of religious service requires only time and persistence. A desire to use worship as a means to cross the invisible line that separates the ordinary from the lofty and exalted, the worldly from the holy, is all that is necessary to feel at home in a synagogue.

Of course, Jews can pray individually, in the privacy of their homes, but according to our tradition, only collective prayer, with at least ten people, ensures the divine presence of God or *Shechinah*.

Jewish religious service follows the order presented in the Siddur, the Jewish book of prayers. On weekdays, the worship starts with introductory prayers: texts from the Torah, from psalms, from books of the prophets, fragments from different religious texts, the wisdom of great teachers of the Jewish religious tradition. After that, the leader of the service calls for the main part of the worship: first a prayer starting with the words *Bar'chu et Adonai ham'vorach* ("Praise the Lord, Who is worthy of all praise"), followed by other prayers, and concluded with the well-known prayer *Sh'ma*, which contains key concepts of monotheism.

Sh'ma (Hear) belongs to one of the most important prayers. The opening words of it, *Sh'ma Yis'ra'eil Adonai Eloheinu Adonai echad* ("Hear, o Israel, the Lord is our God, the Lord the One"), are said by Jews every night before falling asleep. These are the same words a Jew is supposed to utter as death approaches. Many generations of Jews have pronounced the prayer of Sh'ma during the most severe trials of their lives; with the words "*Sh'ma, Yis'ra'eil*," they went to their deaths, when, during their tragic history, they were murdered only for being Jews.

After the prayer Sh'ma and several other prayers, the central part of the worship called *Amidah* or *Shemoneh Ezrei* or Eighteen Benedictions begins. These prayers are to be said standing.

Tachanun, or Supplication, is read after Amidah. It includes a number of additional prayers of entreaty for mercy, protection, and redemption.

With few variations, Kaddish, a prayer praising the holiness of the Lord's name and His might and containing an appeal to God to grant peace thrice, is read several times during the service. A main function of the Kaddish is to separate the different parts of the worship service. Kaddish for the deceased is well-known even to those Jews who come to synagogue infrequently. It is usually read soon after worship begins and again at the end of it.

The Torah reading has been established for centuries and is always a solemn and memorable religious occasion. The Torah is read from the scroll in the synagogue on Mondays, Thursdays, and during the Shabbat services. After a Kaddish is said, a Torah scroll is removed from the Ark where it is stored, and the weekly portion from the Pentateuch is read by the Torah reader. The Torah scroll, which has always been and still is written with a special quill and ink on parchment made from the skin of a kosher animal, starts from the beginning on the holiday of Simchat Torah and is fully completed in a year. A new cycle begins the following year.

When the ceremony of reading the weekly portion of the Torah is completed, several psalms and then the ancient prayer *Aleinu leshabeach* ("It is our duty to praise") are uttered. The worship concludes with the mourner's Kaddish. After that, it is customary for a rabbi to deliver a short sermon dedicated to various religious issues.

During Shabbat, on Saturday, the service is longer than on weekdays. Additional prayers and rituals are added to the afore-mentioned weekday's almost universal structure of worship.

In four different places in the Torah, God prescribes that believers put on *tefillin* (phylacteries) during prayer. Tefillin are two small black leather boxes encapsulating extracts from the Pentateuch written on parchment. By leather straps, one tefillin is placed on the arm and the other is affixed to the head. The sight of a Jew wearing such objects during morning service may surprise and confuse those who are unaware of this commandment, but for religious Jews this is an integral part of the daily worship. Wearing tefillin connects a Jew through the generations to those who stood at Mount Sinai when God gave the Torah to the Jewish nation, to those who prayed at the First and Second Temples in Jerusalem, to the defenders of Masada, to the Maccabeans, to the Jewish nation, which has safely preserved to the present time the decrees God gave them.

In 1969, during excavations in caves in the Judean Desert near the Dead Sea, an archeological team led by famed Israeli archeologist Yigael Yadin found fragments of tefillin dating back to around the first century of the Common Era. The most dramatic discovery was of a two-thousand-year-old head part of tefillin, with each folded inside its appropriate compartment, parchments that contained the prescribed text.

* * *

The initial feeling that religious services last too long disappears when newcomers are able to perceive the contours of the coherent, logical structure of worship. The evolving progress in understanding the meaning of prayers transforms a passive listener into an active participant in a collective appeal to the Almighty. The innermost desire of a human being to bring a lofty sense to the content of prayer makes the process of divine service not only interesting but every time unique.

Unlike other monotheistic religions, in Judaism, clergy do not act as mediator between God and man; when Jews say prayers, they believe that they are on a "direct line" to God.

A rabbi is a teacher and mentor who directs the believers through the unfailing, centuries-old tradition of interpreting religious texts.

A prayer book, or *Siddur*, helps one pray to God in the established tradition, using the same heartfelt and exalted words many generations of Jews have employed while addressing God. In its own way, each *Siddur* is a canon, a golden standard that people employ to express their reverence and gratitude to God. However, in a period assigned for the purpose, worshipers may address God with a personal prayer using their own thoughts and words.

In many synagogues, the services can be conducted by a rabbi or cantor or by a *baal tefillah* (leader of the prayer service)—a lay person familiar with the text and content of the service. In the first months of visiting the synagogue, I could not even imagine how a person like me, with very limited Jewish religious education, could ever lead the worship. However, when I had attended my synagogue for four years, the cantor greatly honored me by offering to prepare me to become a *baal tefillah*.

Over our long history, talented composers, both known and unknown, have set the texts of many prayers to the unforgettable melodies well known to Jews who attend synagogue. These melodies are engraved into people's memory and become an indelible part of their lives. To prepare me to lead weekday services, the cantor sang and recorded on tape the entire content of weekday worship. After months of regular practicing, though I was quite nervous, I went up to the *bimah*—a raised platform in a synagogue for conducting services—to lead the minyan in worship for the first time in my life.

Everyone who has the honor of leading the prayers in the religious service and of reading and handling the Torah scroll is greeted with a handshake accompanied by short but significant phrases, such as "*Yasher koah*" or "*Hazak v'baruch*." "*Yasher koah*" could be translated as "May your strength be firm," and "*Hazak v'baruch*" is said to wish someone to be healthy and blessed. I heard these encouraging phrases from fellow congregants when I finished leading the religious service for the first time.

I understood well the symbolic meaning of what was happening: after skipping a generation with my parents, who had almost completely lost connection with religion, on that unforgettable and very special day, I restored my spiritual connection, and my family's spiritual connection, with the long chain of previous generations.

The original text of prayers is in Hebrew. Most *Siddurs* provide edited translations of the Hebrew text in the language familiar to the reader. This text is usually printed on the page opposite the original Hebrew text. Because of this dual-language format, I knew what a prayer said. Otherwise, with my very limited knowledge of Hebrew, I would hardly have known the literal meaning of the separate words and phrases. In a way, though, I felt unsatisfied. Although God probably always knows what they are about, prayers are considered more effective when a person praying understands what he or she says. Because I wanted to know the exact meaning of prayers, I began to actively study Hebrew.

The morning service is called *Shacharit* ("morning light" in Hebrew), the afternoon service is called *Minha*, and the evening service is *Ma'ariv*. Shacharit lasts relatively longer than the other two services. The Torah is read directly from the scroll three days of the week and also on religious holidays and *Rosh Chodesh*, the beginning of each lunar month.

Reading from the Torah scroll is one of the most solemn parts of the worship. Faithful Jews consider it their privilege and duty to be present when they have an opportunity to hear the living words of God.

While three portions of text from the Torah are read on weekdays, during the Shabbat service the reading from the Torah usually is divided into seven parts. Almost always, before and after the Torah reading, there is a solemn procession. A congregant carries the Torah around the synagogue in his arms. As the Torah passes the other congregants, they touch the cover with their hands or with a prayer book or their tallit and then kiss whatever they touched the Torah with. After the Torah reading, while the congregational response is recited (*v'zot ha-Torah*. . .), the Torah holder raises the Torah up high with its text facing the congregation.

Anyone present can ask for the honor of an *aliah*—an opportunity to be called up either to read the Torah or to stand next to the Torah reader, who chants the text directly from the scroll. Before and after the Torah reading, a special prayer is said.

VISITING RABBI MENACHEM
MENDEL SCHNEERSON

EVERY NEW GENERATION of Jewish people has its great sages who, in their attempt to approach the divine truth, leave their indelible legacy in the history of Judaism. I was fortunate to meet one such great sage and teacher. This encounter helped me understand more about the continuity of great traditions intrinsic to the Jewish religion. In 1986, my wife and I went to New York to attend a *farbrengen* (Yiddish meaning: "joyous gathering") held by the world-famous leader of the Lubavitch movement, Rabbi Menachem Mendel Schneerson. As usual, the farbrengen took place in the legendary Lubavitch synagogue located in the famous 770 Eastern Parkway building in Brooklyn, New York.

I was shocked by the contrast between what was familiar to me in the Soviet Union and what I saw at that time in America. In the U.S.S.R., the Soviet authorities constantly reminded the Jews that they owed their right to breathe to the Communist Party. Being objects of continuous official and unofficial persecution and humiliation, Jews in the U.S.S.R tried by all means not to "advertise" their Jewishness and— as much as possible—avoided drawing attention to their ethnic origin. And now, after all my previous experience, here in New York, unexpectedly, I saw my people joyous and happy, living a strong spiritual life and practicing Judaism with unapologetic enthusiasm. They wore Hasidic clothes; they did not try to seem invisible like many of their fellow Jews living in the Soviet state; they walked with their heads raised high, proud to belong to the Jewish nation. Also new to me was the high intensity of sincere religious feelings and the demonstration of ardent faith in God, which I had never had an opportunity to observe before and which people of the free world take for granted.

In his popular book *9½ Mystics*, Rabbi Herbert Weiner describes his very long conversation with Rabbi Schneerson. Among other questions, he asked Rabbi Schneerson why all the Hasidim in his synagogue looked so determined and confident. Smiling, Rabbi Schneerson answered that, unlike the people of modern society who live in two sharply contrasting worlds, the secular and the spiritual, his Hasidim live in one world, in the world of eternal spiritual values.

It is a common opinion that, because he was a man of immense personal power, Rabbi Schneerson could make his interviewer feel as if he had somehow foreseen meeting them and during the conversation, it was as if all his attention was focused on discussing any burning questions that his visitor brought.

The great personal power and charisma of the rabbi—which I observed myself—combined with the wisdom of a sage, had an enormous historical influence on the lives of Jews both in the US and throughout the world.

Starting in the 1950s, he developed the idea of *shluchim*, or emissaries—members of the religious movement sent out not to proselytize but to promulgate Judaism and to assist Jews and Jewish communities worldwide in their religious needs.

Nowadays, shluchim can even be found in many of the most remote places in the world. As of 2010 there were about 4,500 of the rabbi's emissaries worldwide. On November 2, 1994, Rabbi Schneerson, who combined the qualities of a world class leader with true humanity, was posthumously awarded a Congressional Gold Medal.

During the *farbrengen* in the New York, the spacious hall of the synagogue was filled with thousands of Hasidim standing very close to one another; their heads covered with black hats seen from above gave the impression of the waves of a rolling sea.

If in the country of my birth Jews were second-rate citizens; here I saw my people free, able to follow the ideals set forth in the Torah purposefully and openly.

As a general on a battlefield, the gray-haired, life-asserting rabbi stood on the podium and conducted the religious service with his hand, confidently leading his army of Hasidim disciples to achieve the desired goal—to draw God's attention to the prayers of His faithful children.

For Rabbi Schneerson and the members of his movement, God was not a dry, abstract theological precept subject to any kind of capricious interpretation, but a living God, always actively involved in the personal fates of the people of the world.

Rabbi Schneerson addressed the audience in Yiddish. It was impossible not to feel the strength of the penetrating expression of his eagle eyes, and the rabbi's glance gave the impression that he could see the future. From time to time during the service, he gazed into the faces of his followers, giving a sensation that he possessed the ability to read human souls. The Hasidim caught every word of their teacher's sermon, steadily expressing their great enthusiasm for his speech. With a slight raise of his hand, the rabbi from time to time gave them a sign, and the audience broke forth with the sounds of a new prayer. Rabbi Schneerson sang with his followers, energetically conducting them with his clenched fist.

Judging by the reaction of those present, Rabbi Schneerson served as a bridge capable of uniting them with heaven and with God Himself.

Jews from America and from around the world who believed in the vision and wisdom of the rabbi came to share important news with him, get vital advice, or receive blessings when they had to make important decisions about their destinies.

Many books have been written about the enormous personal power of Rabbi Schneerson, but nothing can compare the experience of meeting him personally. In order to speak with him, one had to stand in a long line beginning far outside the building and ending at the door of the rabbi's office. When our turn came to see the rabbi, he was standing near the open door of his study. He was full of energy and sincere care for the people who came to meet him.

A man of respectable age with a bushy gray beard, he greeted us warmly, as if we were his old friends. Somehow the rabbi easily understood the reason for our visit. Looking at us intently from under his thick eyebrows he patiently waited until we finished our story, and then gave us advice, the meaning of which was totally beyond our understanding. Nevertheless, following his completely unexpected recommendation for our critical situation, amazingly, we were able to resolve our problem. Thus, we joined many people in whose lives Rabbi Schneerson's legendary advice worked miracles.

The unforgettable meeting with Rabbi Schneerson had important consequences in our life.

From the moment of our arrival in the US, my wife had a job that allowed her to be free on Saturdays. For me, however, being a physician, I thought I would not be able to avoid working on Saturdays, because my patients might need urgent care.

However, after meeting with the rabbi, I firmly decided to stop working on Saturdays.

It turned out to be much easier than I expected. According to Judaism, which is a religion dedicated to worshipping God's creation and is alien to fanaticism, there is nothing more precious than a human life. This is illustrated by the main principle of Judaism: "*pikuach nefesh*," roughly translated as "the preservation of human life."

In exceptional circumstances, when only a particular doctor can render urgent medical care to a patient, and this involvement is critically important for saving life, a believer, in this case a practicing physician, can temporarily—for the period necessary to render medical aid—break the devotional religious duty to abstain from work on Saturdays and religious holidays.

Shabbat observance brought remarkable changes to our family life. It is one thing just to consider yourself a Jew, but it is quite another to join the lifestyle prescribed by the Torah, with the awareness that observance of the main commandments of Judaism is not a burden but, on the contrary, a source of profound joy and inner satisfaction. Those who keep Shabbat—the Day of Eternity—can, at least once a week, escape from the everyday material world full of numerous empty temptations and discover the boundless world of spiritual values. Abstinence from daily work enables believers to live a spiritual life and, to put it figuratively, to communicate with heaven, from the moment of lighting the Shabbat candles on Friday evening until sunset of the next day.

The stricter observance of Shabbat led our family to more meticulous observance of Jewish dietary laws. Many Jewish theologians, including the great teacher Moses Maimonides, wrote that the kosher rules are not a capricious set of laws, but a rational and logical realization of the principles of hygiene and healthy diet.

The Chinese say, "Every long journey begins with a single step." Conducting a small revolution in our household proved to be easier than we had expected. Widely available literature on the subject of *kashrut* and the advice of our religious friends helped us to understand thoroughly the basic requirements of the dietary laws. Besides designated sets of kitchen dishes for meat and milk products, we also bought a separate assortment of them for the celebration of Passover and obtained the necessary items for conducting rituals related to meals.

The good news for us was that kosher products were easily available in different areas of Chicago and in practically all large cities in the US.

THE TORAH, HAPHTARAH, THEOLOGY, AND TRADITION

READING A WEEKLY CHAPTER from the Torah is one of the central moments of worship.

As previously mentioned, the Torah is read three times a week in the synagogue: on Saturdays, Mondays, and Thursdays. It is also read on Jewish holidays and at the beginning of each lunar month.

In the handwritten Torah scroll, there are no punctuation marks, no vowels to prompt the reader to the exact meaning of each word, no beginning to each new sentence, verse, or chapter; also absent are special marks indicating with what particular melody each single word or group of words of the Scripture has to be chanted. It takes many years of dedicated preparation and long and strenuous effort to read the Torah scroll accurately and without mistakes, as well as to render its musical content.

Within a year, the whole text of the Torah is read in succession from beginning to end. During cantillation from the scroll, another person who has mastered the Torah stands next to the reader, to make sure that the reader makes no mistakes in pronouncing either the text or the tropes—melodies set to the text. Cantillation is the ritual chanting of readings from the Bible in synagogue services. The chants are written and notated in accordance with the special signs or marks printed in the Masoretic text of the Bible (or *Tanakh*) to complement the letters and vowel points.

While chanting the Torah requires special skills, those who wish to take an active role in the religious service will find that it is much easier to learn how to read the Haphtarah—a weekly passage from the books of Biblical prophets recited on Shabbat and religious holidays immediately after the Torah service. The content of the Haphtarah is usually associated with either the weekly text of the Torah or with the special religious event of the week. The Haphtarah also has its own musical standards, different from the Torah, which are accepted throughout the Jewish world. The Haphtarah is read from a separate scroll or, more frequently, from a book and is much easier to chant than the Torah, thanks to the symbols of vowels, punctuation marks, and musical signs marked in the text. The chanting of Haphtarah involves about fifteen main musical tropes, each of which consists of a fixed combination of several musical sounds. Like building blocks, tropes help to put together a unique melody for each word and sentence.

It did not take too long for the cantor in my synagogue to teach me the musical subtleties of cantillation, and, to my own surprise, I managed to chant my first Haphtarah. By then I was participating in the religious service long enough to comprehend Hebrew text. The ability to chant Haphtarah provided me with inner satisfaction, because it symbolized another step towards learning the living religious tradition of Judaism.

* * *

Until the last few centuries, Jewish theologians, unlike Christians, did not show much interest in the philosophy of religion. The majority of religious Jews were not interested in philosophy, because from their point of view, a philosophy of religion could offer nothing; for them, the existence of God has always been a self-evident, *a priori* truth, an axiom not requiring additional substantiation. God had already found Jews and the Jews had found God; all that remained was to look for ways of getting closer to Him by learning the Torah, the Talmud, books of Jewish sages, by offering up prayers to God, and by making the world more perfect by performing good deeds for Him, for Jews, and for the entire human race.

In contrast to other religions, Judaism is concentrated not on the hereafter but on earthly existence and, above all, on the institution of the family.

While the inevitable conclusion of atheism is that human life is just a random event, culminating in the total disappearance of the person from the face of the earth, Judaism attaches high spiritual meaning to the life of every individual: each human being is born to this world to fulfill a uniquely important earthly mission during his or her life. The life of every Jew is dedicated to the service of God, family, the Jewish people, and the whole human race. Jews believe in *Tikkun Olam* ("repairing the world" in Hebrew) and consider it their duty to actively participate in the improvement and perfection of the world—an activity they will account for when their turn comes to appear before the throne of God. Religious Jews wholly dedicate themselves to the observance of religious ethics and to living a pure, sinless-as-possible life.

The fact that most religious Jews agree on the basic problems of existence does not mean that they do not have many conflicting views on certain issues.

This is illustrated in a popular Jewish joke: in one of the synagogues are two constantly conflicting factions. One of them claims that everyone should stand up when the Sh'ma prayer is read, while the other insists that everyone should remain seated. In order to solve the dispute, the congregants decide to ask the advice of the oldest member of the synagogue, who by now lives in a nursing home.

They ask him what the synagogue's tradition was regarding saying the Sh'ma prayer.

"First tell me what's going on in the synagogue these days," asks the elder.

They tell the old man that those who stand up during the Sh'ma prayer grumble and nod their heads disapprovingly at those who remain seated; as for those who sit, they shake their heads in objection to those who stand up.

At this moment the old man raises his index finger with significance and announces categorically, "Oh! That's it! That's the tradition of our synagogue: some are standing, others are sitting, and both disagree."

COME TO YOUR HOME

DURING ONE OF MY MEETINGS with a leading rabbi of Chicago at the Russian Lubavitch congregation, I expressed my disappointment that so few of our countrymen take advantage of the opportunity they did not have before they came to the US: to become a member of the synagogue of their choice. Even more disappointing is that some of our landsmen cut ties with Judaism forever, and even express hostility toward those who profess the religion of their fathers.

"I think that no one should be judged too strictly," the rabbi answered in a mild and polite manner. "The Lubavitch movement believes that since in every Jew lives a *yiddishe neshome* [the Jewish spirit], nothing will make Jews abandon their traditions, their roots, their destiny forever. Sooner or later 'the still-quiet voice' of their Jewish hearts will tell them that their place is among those who continue to practice the religion and traditions of their fathers."

In Canada we have a distant relative whose name is Hannah. Her parents are well-to-do people who are totally indifferent to any religion. In the 1970s, when Hannah was nineteen, her friends introduced her to Hinduism and persuaded her to go to India for "spiritual enrichment."

Hannah liked India so much she settled there permanently in an ashram. She lived on the money her parents sent her regularly. In addition, she made a small income by giving English lessons to local schoolchildren. Once a year she returned to Canada, where she would stay for four to six weeks with her parents and friends.

At one of the family reunions, I found myself her neighbor at the table. Hannah was good company, so we soon became involved in conversation. Gradually our talk shifted to religious topics.

Surprisingly, Hannah did not mind this subject. On the contrary, she seemed pleased to have a conversation about Judaism and listened with interest when I told her that, like Hinduism, the religion of her fathers also includes vast materials on religious mysticism. I also told her about the worldwide popularity of the ancient Jewish teaching, the Kabbalah, the heritage left by legendary Jewish mystics, and the important place of meditation in Judaism.

"I know how important it is for you to satisfy your need for spiritual enrichment, and that is, I guess, why Hinduism attracts you," I told her. "But I would like you to know that what you are trying to find in another religion, on another continent, among strangers, abounds in your own religion, awaits you at your home, is ready for you to explore. Why travel to India, if here, in Toronto—where you are from— there is an unlimited opportunity to get acquainted with what Judaism says about the things you are interested in?"

"I don't doubt it. I am sure that I could have been a good Jew," Hannah answered, "but when I was growing up nobody spoke to me about religion. I have never denied that I'm Jewish; I have read much about the Holocaust and worldwide anti-Semitism, and I always took great interest in what was happening in Israel. I love my parents very much, but they have never shown any interest in religion. They still think that being a Jew means belonging to the common culture and common history but not the common religion of the Jewish people. I can't live in a vacuum; I have always had an urge to search for the meaning of life. For me—it's the way I am—it is very important to believe, so I chose Hinduism. Though this does not mean that I reject Judaism, I'm now too old to change. Judaism is unfamiliar to me and, to be honest, it's more alien than close to me."

"I understand that perfectly well, Hannah, but if for no other reason than just curiosity, couldn't you find a little time to get better acquainted with what our people have lived for so many centuries?" I interjected.

"I've lived in India for such a long time," she answered, "that Judaism seems to have left me. It remains forever in my past life. Besides, it doesn't matter to my family what I do. The only thing they want to know is that I am alive and well, the rest is of little interest to them. I went to synagogue only when I was a child—my grandparents took me there."

"I don't blame my parents," she added. "I love them very much, I do, but they have always lived for today and always admitted that religion was not at all important to them."

* * *

Several years have passed since my conversation with Hannah. She still spends most of her time in India, where this very intelligent woman, who grew up in a free world, apparently lives not thinking for herself but following the advice of her guru. Like an obedient schoolgirl, of her own will, she allows a person foreign to the values of her people to control her life.

I have heard too many arguments from my Jewish friends and acquaintances trying to explain their estrangement from religion. The young say that they are too young for religion, the middle-aged claim that they are in the process of making their decision, the elderly offer the excuse that they are too old to start spiritual life. The people who reverently listen to rabbis' sermons when they are invited to a synagogue for weddings, Bar and Bat Mitzvah ceremonies, and other significant events, when asked why they otherwise never attend synagogue, smile shyly and come up with all kinds of excuses and explanations.

Meanwhile, these people find enough time to visit theaters and concert halls, see movies, travel all over the world, attend sports events, spend long hours in restaurants and at endless parties.

There are numerous things they spend their free time on, but, unfortunately, for some reason, they have no time for mankind's most important activity—connecting their spiritual selves with eternity.

Judaism contains an inexhaustible wealth of knowledge, where there is room for any interest, method, or approach. The only action necessary to discover this ancient but ever-new religion is to open the door leading to the perception of truth. The tree of knowledge of our four-thousand-year-old religion is widespread and boundless. This freedom of thought led so many generations of our people's best intellects to dedicate their lives to comprehending the ideals of our religion, for which they were prepared to undergo any trials and tribulations.

WITH A PRAYER
IN THEIR HEARTS

THERE ARE DIFFERENT METHODS of introducing readers who do not know Hebrew to Hebrew religious texts. For many centuries, this was done by positioning a translation on the opposite page from, or sometimes below, the original Hebrew text.

In the twentieth century, interlinear translations emerged. They break the original text into small phrases, the meanings of which appear separate columns. This was a significant step toward enabling the reader to better understand what is said in the Torah and prayers.

Not long ago another valuable innovation occurred in the presentation of Hebrew text. The US publisher Art Scroll Machzor published interlinear translations of the Pentateuch and many Siddurim. In interlinear translation, every single Hebrew word has printed under it the English translation in the appropriate grammatical and syntactic form. As a result, readers unfamiliar with Hebrew and without special religious education can learn exactly what is said in the Torah or in prayer books.

In addition to the interlinear translation, Art Scroll Machzor prints on the same page commentaries to the text by famous teachers of Judaism, such as Rashi, Nachmanides,

Onkelos, and Maimonides, making it much easier for the modern reader to comprehend otherwise difficult-to-understand episodes and events of the Bible.

Furthermore, the interlinear method of translation gives the reader the precious opportunity to understand what the literal text says, as well as a solid introduction to the Hebrew language—a language which God spoke, either directly or through His prophets, with the Jewish people.

A prayer is more effective when the worshiper does not automatically repeat the text after the leader of the service speaks it. Interlinear translations of the Siddurim allow people with insufficient knowledge of Hebrew to understand the exact meaning of the words they use in their conversations with God, which adds spiritual satisfaction to their worship.

Ironically, it was not the Conservative or Reform movements of Judaism, who both claim to be more progressive, but the Orthodox movement that provided books to help novices in their religious education.

Every prayer included in the Siddurim has its own meaning and history, sometimes dating back to the time when the first and the second temples in Jerusalem were destroyed. Thanks to the availability of literal translations of the text of the prayers, praying acquires new significance, and many formerly mysterious Hebrew words are soon understood. The time spent in worship passes much more quickly when it is associated with the creative process of acquiring new knowledge.

In prayer, a worshiper who understands the text learns and is more connected to the heartfelt words Jews have used throughout history to address the source of life—Almighty God.

For millennia prayers have helped generations of people to make contact with their deepest spiritual aspirations. It is difficult to imagine living without religion once it becomes an integral part of one's life. Prayer is perhaps the most deeply human response to mundane tribulations. It offers comfort and respite from daily stress by some mechanism that is not yet understood but has been confirmed by numerous medical studies.

Not everyone possesses the self-discipline and inspiration of strictly observant Jews—the soldiers of religion—who follow the smallest details of Jewish Law (*Halacha*). There are Jews who use only specific kosher products, who, in scrupulous observance of kosher laws, have kitchens equipped with separate refrigerators and dishwashers for meat and dairy products. And there are also believers who are not so careful to observe dietary laws.

There are Jews who cannot imagine their life without a regular visit to the *mikvah* (a pool for ritual ablution), while others may never even have heard the word "mikvah." In other words, there are many shades and nuances in Judaism.

For a modern, educated Jew, faith in God is based not only on empirical, intuitive feeling but also on information about constantly widening scientific achievements.

Although a man is destined never to know the absolute truths of being, the inquisitive human mind will never give up attempts to understand them. Every significant new scientific discovery raises fresh questions that broaden the horizon of our knowledge. It is very important to remember that, unlike Christianity and Islam, Judaism has never seen a rival in science; quite to the contrary, Judaism has always welcomed the study of science.

In the Middle Ages, the famous teacher of Judaism, Moses Maimonides, in his work "Guide for the Perplexed" (*Moreh Nevukhimin*, in Hebrew), spoke about the centuries-old tradition of harmony between Judaism and science, urging his readers to respect and carefully study the achievements of scientists.

The scope of the study of Judaism is inexhaustible. It encompasses discovering new horizons of the Bible as well as learning Halacha, the Jewish Law, getting familiar with the mystical teachings of the Kabbalah, studying works by teachers and men of wisdom, such as Rashi, Onkelos, Maimonides, Yehuda ha-Levi, Moshe Chaim Luzzato, Hofez Haim, Menachem Mendel Schneerson, Eliezer Berkovich, Abraham Heschel, Eshiyahu Leibowitz, and many others.

THE STARRY SKIES

HESTER PANIM—"God hides His face"—is one of the concepts of Judaism. Incomprehensibly for us, He rules the world and performs miracles; He participates in everyday matters; He is omnipresent. But His face is hidden from the human race.

No logic, no truth, probably not even a personal encounter with God, can persuade the most zealous atheists to change their minds about their unbelief. Modern militant atheists—and the number of them is constantly increasing in Western society—like medieval inquisitors, do not disdain to use any absurd argument to drown the rational voice of religion. A while ago, a TV show host asked one of these atheists why he so passionately and harshly fought against religion. He answered that he must be aggressive because, as he thinks, the vast majority of those who participate in religious services are not believers but actually atheists, and they come to pray in order to impress others or out of habit. Hence, he feels morally obliged to help these "lost souls" to come to their senses and honestly admit their atheism.

Most believers were brought up in traditional religious families. Some, who grew up without religion and came to faith in God, were intuitively guided by their inner voice, by their belief in the high and transcendental meaning of our fleeting human lives, and by innate perception of the eternal spirit.

The Industrial Revolution was one of the main forces that weakened the faith in God that had prevailed for many millennia. The introduction of countless mechanical and electric machines to everyday life, together with revolutionary achievements in chemistry and biology, was able to create a false impression of earthly immortality overshadowing the truth of human existence.

About fifteen years ago, it became very popular to look for the Bible Codes, which, from the point of view of those who believed in them, miraculously confirmed past events. Several popular books were written about the importance of Bible Codes in allegedly predicting the future. Being intrigued, I attended a symposium called "Discovery" that was held in one of Chicago's suburban hotels. At the final lecture, in a packed hall, a young Jewish lecturer dressed in traditional Orthodox clothes stood in a front of a big screen with an extract from the Torah projected on it. The lecturer pointed at the historical names and events in the passage that he believed reflected what had already happened and even what might happen but would not be recognized until after the occurrence of the events. The audience listened with intense interest. After the lecture was over and the audience began asking questions, the presenter himself respectfully addressed the white-haired leader of Chicago Yeshiva (an Orthodox Jewish college or seminary), who was present in the audience:

"Rabbi, so what do you think about the Bible Codes?"

"Well, what you told us sounds interesting," the rabbi responded after a little thought. Then he continued, "But there is not much to it. I do not think that to prove the existence of God it is worth spending all that time on computer research. It is sufficient to look at the night sky, to see all the ocean of the celestial bodies, to believe in the creator of the universe."

The Industrial Revolution has turned the life of the typical modern person into a twenty-four-hour-a-day entertainment. Spending a substantial part of his life watching television, attending movies, surfing the Internet, playing computer games, this pre-programmed person lives not his own life but the lives of unending characters from the shows he watches. He constantly distracts himself from thinking about the purpose of his own life and the sad fact that the celebration called "life" sooner or later will end. When finally the time comes to leave this world, many people repeat the same cliché so familiar from books, movies, and personal experience: "My God," they say. "How did this happen? Life passed so fast, I did not even have time to really live." Unfortunately, on most days of their lives, people waste plenty of time on trivial things instead of trying to reach the bottomless well of spiritual wealth.

How many people, how many Jews, would be able to fill their lives with cosmic purpose and acquire a strong belief in the uniqueness, importance, and inimitability of their lives if—even for a short time—they could escape from the hypnosis of endless amusements and try to get in touch with their eternal spirit? The ever-present conflict between believers and nonbelievers will be solved only after the coming of the long-awaited Messiah, but before this happens the majority of people will choose to have faith in God, following the inner voice of their hearts.

During a discussion between believers and atheists, the latter often resort to the argument that if God really existed there would be no evil in the world, people would not kill one another, and there would be no violence or bloody wars.

Atheists are sincerely surprised to learn that Judaism has never turned a blind eye to the existence of evil. The question of why terrible, unfair tragedies happen to good people has always been one of the main subjects of discussion by monotheistic theologians. Throughout the long history of mankind, a vast number of religious works have been dedicated to this subject.

There have been numerous attempts to explain the presence of evil. Some of these attempts seem to approach the truth, while others are not as persuasive. There is no final explanation of why evil exists, and religion has never made a secret of that. Yet failure to explain evil does not deter believers from their unshakable faith in God. This is because the unsolved mystery of evil in the world is outweighed by the rest of human experience. A few decades ago, well-known American theologian Milton Steinberg said on this subject: "The believer in God has to account for the existence of unjust suffering; the atheist has to account for everything else."

A favorite argument of atheists against religion is the history of religious wars and various acts of brutality perpetrated in the name of God. It is necessary to note here that, for at least two thousand years, Judaism has not been involved in acts of violence. Meanwhile, atheists do not consider the fact that the number of victims of religious wars does not come close to the enormous number of lives lost as a result of the crimes of twentieth-century atheist regimes. If in religious wars and persecutions hundreds of thousands of lives were lost, non-religious, atheistic wars claimed the lives of hundreds of millions: the non-religious First and Second World Wars left seventy million dead. Nine million were killed during the 1917 revolution in Russia, while the number of victims of Stalin's terror is estimated to be between twenty and forty million. In China, more than forty million people died under Mao Tse Tung between 1949 and 1975. Pol Pot's regime in Cambodia killed two million Cambodians. In Rwanda 1.6 million were annihilated as a result of tribal wars, while the number of victims in Congo was four million. This is an incomplete list of the victims of atheist regimes during the twentieth century.

A believer dedicates his life to getting closer to God, serving Him, and understanding His essence. Judaism is one of the most democratic and accessible religions: nothing and nobody stand between a man and God. Each faithful Jew professes religion at a level that he or she thinks appropriate. The broad tolerance of Judaism is illustrated by the fact that, unique to this religion, a person born to a Jewish mother continues to be Jewish even if he or she has serious doubts about the existence of God. People sharing and believing in the principles of Judaism who really wish to become Jews can do so regardless of their race or skin color.

The study of the Torah is a spiritually enriching occupation, full of uppermost and unique meaning and sense. Judaism is an inexhaustible repository of learning. A great number of works provide detailed interpretations and commentary on the text of the Five Books of Moses. Apart from the better-known written and oral Torahs, the books of prophets, the Talmud with commentary, and the mystical teachings of the Kabbalah, there is a vast amount of literature created by the great Jewish sages, rabbis, and theologians, of both ancient and modern times, covering all possible aspects of Judaism.

AND ONE MORE MIRACLE

In this book, I have described events in my life that I have delegated to the category of miracles. When this book was almost finished, another miracle occurred that I ought to share with my readers.

In synagogues and various Jewish organizations, I periodically heard that in the United States there are many Christians who are not only steadfast and uncompromising supporters of the State of Israel but who also consider the Jewish people to be their brothers and sisters in religious and historical destiny.

Four years ago, I was pleasantly surprised to learn about the existence of the International Fellowship of Christians and Jews established in 1983 by the Chicago Rabbi Yechiel Eckstein. This organization has been dispensing charity in the form of food, clothes, and humanitarian aid to needy Jews throughout the world, particularly in Israel and the former Soviet Union.

Only at the beginning of 2011 did I learn about another organization dedicated to solidarity with Israel, "Christians United for Israel" (CUFI), which ardently and consistently defends the interests of the Jewish people and the State of Israel on both religious and political levels. Like the hero of Ivan Andreevich Krylov's fable, "The Curious," who got so carried away with little insects at the Museum of Curiosities that he did not notice an elephant, I did not suspect that a powerful, organized Christian Zionist movement existed in the US. Later I found out that Christian Zionists, who always held on to the belief that the Jewish people, after thousands years of exile, would return to Israel, to the land that was given to them by God, have existed since the time of the Reformation.

In his autobiography *Trial and Error* published in 1949, Chaim Weizmann, the first President of Israel, narrates in detail how, after he had several meetings with British political leaders who were practicing Christians, including Prime Minister Lloyd George and Lord Balfour, on November 5, 1917, the British government issued the historic Balfour Declaration, the document forming the legal and moral foundation for fulfillment of the dream of Jewish people for thousands of years: reestablishment of the Jewish state in the ancient land of Israel.

Since we had heard a lot of contradictory opinions about American Christian Zionists, my wife and I decided to find out for ourselves who the Christian Zionists really were. In July 2011, an opportunity presented itself: a three-day national CUFI Summit held in Washington, D.C.

What we saw and heard exceeded our boldest expectations. The summit took place in a central conference hall in Washington with five thousand delegates participating— Christians from all denominations, including Catholic, Baptist, and Pentecostal, but mostly Evangelical. There was also a small group of religious and non-religious Jews from the US and Israel.

Because of my life experience, what I saw and heard was impossible to believe. I met not a small fringe group but a multitude of Christians from different denominations who considered Jewish people not forgotten and forsaken by God, not blamed for refusing to believe in Jesus, but worthy, equal brothers and partners in monotheism, people who fully deserve to be respected and who have the unconditional legitimate right to consider the State of Israel their national historical home.

A book fair was organized on one of the floors of the building. After standing in a rather long line, we finally reached the book stalls and could look through the displays. And here, we were to make another discovery: it turns out that a great number of books written by Christians and published in this country cover different aspects of Jewish religious and nonreligious life and reflect on the State of Israel in a serious and truly positive manner.

Once I had a next-door neighbor, a well-known Christian preacher, who definitely sympathized with the State of Israel. His name was Robert. We were real friends, visited and helped each other many times. He was very familiar with Jewish sources and we often discussed the Bible, analyzing its contents as we compared Judaism and Christianity. Since we had surprisingly close views on many religious issues and on our faith in God, I could say that I felt more spiritual closeness to him than to my atheist Jewish friends.

Alas, our firm friendship ended abruptly one day.

"Robert, in the long run, religion is an individual choice," I said to him that day. "I am a Jew, you are a Christian, but God will reward us in equal measure for our merits, which I hope we both possess."

"It's not as simple as you think," Robert replied with a totally unexpected and undisguised air of superiority. "Don't forget, Vladimir, that those who do not believe in Jesus Christ cannot expect salvation."

"So you think that after death I will go to hell? Is that so?"

Robert was silent.

"And what about the innocent children, and more than one billion Chinese and Hindu—are they all destined for hell? They have never heard about Jesus!"

"The Christianity I preach believes that only those who accept Jesus Christ as a personal savior might hope to receive intercession before God and absolution of their sins," my long time friend answered firmly with an apologetic smile.

During the CUFI Summit, we encountered nothing similar to my former neighbor's attitude. Everyone we met at the summit spoke to us with genuine and natural respect and did their best to make us feel at home. The participants of the summit would have found a question like "Why did the Jews crucify Jesus?" totally out of place, offensive and inappropriate.

They treated Jews who attended the summit as brothers in faith, as members of one big family of mankind, as people with whom they shared a belief in one God, creator of the universe. While I was among my newly acquired friends, the words of "Joyful, Joyful, We Adore Thee," which Henry Van Dyke put to "Ode to Joy" in Beethoven's Ninth Symphony, came to my mind:

Joyful, joyful, we adore Thee, God of glory, Lord of love;
Hearts unfold like flowers before Thee, opening to the
    sun above.
Melt the clouds of sin and sadness; drive the dark of
    doubt away;

Giver of immortal gladness, fill us with the light of day!

Mortals, join the happy chorus, which the morning
    stars began;
Father love is reigning o'er us, brother love binds man
    to man.
Ever singing, march we onward, victors in the midst
    of strife,
Joyful music leads us Sunward in the triumph song of life.

For any Jew familiar with the persecution of Jewish people
by Christians since the fourth century, it would be natural to
suspect a Christian who extends to him a hand of friendship
of insincerity. However, it is absolutely impossible that all five
thousand Christians gathered in Washington from all over the
US, who spent their own time and money to be there, came
just to pretend that they support the Jewish people and Israel.

The CUFI organization was founded by the famous pastor and orator John Hagee of San Antonio, Texas, in 2006
and currently has more than one million members.

One of the remarkable acquaintances we made during
the congress was Pastor Sam Whaley from Spindale, North
Carolina. His family and all the members of his church—several hundred people—came with him to Washington. In one
of the halls of the building where the summit took place was a
huge memorial called The Holocaust Museum and an exhibi-
tion about the history of Israel; both were created by Whaley's
church as a tribute to the Jewish people and the State of Israel.
Among many other exhibits there were perfect models of the
Mishkan—tabernacles built by Moses in the desert according

to the instructions given to him by God—and of the Second Temple in Jerusalem, Beit HaMikdash.

The Holocaust Museum exhibit offered numerous paintings, sculptures, and reproductions of documents relevant to the theme. Though made by amateurs, many items in the exposition looked very professional. I saw people overwhelmed by the emotional and moral power of the display.

One of the speakers at the summit was the famous public leader, author, and political commentator Glenn Beck. His speech was worthy of inclusion in the annals of the history of Christian-Jewish relations.

In his speech, which was charged with strong emotion, Beck warned enemies of Israel and of the Jewish people that times had changed and that the Jews would not be alone in any confrontation with modern followers of Hitler. Standing up for Israel "may be the cause of our lifetime. . . Each of us will be judged as a people and a nation by how we treat Israel.

"If a despised regime [decides] to kill Jews and frighten those who stand with them, I declare," he said, "count me a Jew and come for me first! When we all stand together, when we all raise our hands, we change the world. They cannot kill all of us. Let us declare: I am a Jew!"

At this point, all five thousand participants of the congress rose to their feet and the room erupted with thunderous applause. Glenn Beck continued, "Our Jewish friends must all know that those who wish them harm must be warned. This still is America. We are not the Christians of the Crusades; we are the Christians United for Israel!"

During registration on the first day of the summit, we found ourselves standing next to a nice-looking elderly woman who wore a beautiful brooch made in the form of the Hebrew word יי ("life") on her jacket. We started to talk. The woman and her husband were from Atlanta, Georgia. Having guessed by our Russian accents where we came from, they asked when we had arrived in the United States.

"Oh, at the end of 1974?" said the woman, whose name was Pamela. "What a coincidence! At the beginning of 1974, Senators Henry Jackson and Charles Vanik fought for the adoption of their bill, which denied normal trade relations between the US and countries, like the Soviet Union, that restricted emigration and violated other human rights. The amendment was implemented later. But in the early months of 1974, practically all the members of our congregation went to Washington to support the Jews living in the now former Soviet Union—like you—in their wish to emigrate."

"So your efforts were not wasted," my wife said. "As a matter of fact we are the Jews you fought for. Without your help we would probably not be here today. Thank you from the bottom of our hearts."

"Come on! You don't need to thank us. We did what we thought was the right thing to do. By the way, you seem to like my favorite Hebrew brooch. I bought it in Washington in 1974 at the Smithsonian."

"I thought this support started only after the 9/11 tragedy, when American Christians saw the parallels between their own fate and the fate of Jews in the Middle East," I said. "I didn't know that American Christians have supported the Jewish people for such a long time."

"Indeed, you were mistaken," Pam said. "I grew up in a Christian family and my parents always told me that anyone who believes in the Bible should respect and honor the Jewish people. However, not all Christians are the same; there are

Christians in the US who do not hide their hatred for Jews. But America is a big country, and I'm sure that there are many more Christians who sympathize with the plight of Jewish people and the State of Israel than who are their enemies."

During one of the sessions, I asked if the CUFI organization was addressing the progressively worsening problem of the persecution of Christians in the Middle East.

"For instance," I said, "over the past few years, many Christians have been leaving Bethlehem, the birthplace of Jesus, because of discrimination and maltreatment."

I was told that CUFI specifically focuses on supporting Israel and fighting anti-Semitism, and that the plight of Christians in the Middle East is taken care of by other Christian organizations.

Exceptions prove the rule. One short encounter during the summit provoked undesirable emotions and associations. On the second day of the summit, a young Christian man from Minnesota, whose name was Tom, approached me. Because I had a kippah (skull cap) on my head, he knew I was Jewish, and he expressed his strong desire to know my opinion on some issues that allegedly interested him.

"First of all, do you realize that this conference is far from being a typical Christian event?" With this phrase, so strange under the circumstances, Tom started the conversation.

"Do you know," he continued, "that there are many Christians in America who do not support Israel and really hate Jewish people?"

"There are many anti-Semites in America," Tom repeated more than once.

"You do not need to remind me about it. I am much more aware of it than you." I was forced to interrupt the unnecessary and out-of-place remarks of my interlocutor. "That's exactly why I am here: to be reassured and receive evidence that, in spite of the bad things, in this country there are many Christians who, for whatever reason, give their ardent support to the Jewish people."

"So I want you to explain to me," Tom, who was sticking to his guns, asked me with an innocent air, "why are the Jews hated so much?"

"Does that really interest you, or have you for some reason decided to test my knowledge on this issue?"

"Yes, yes, yes!" Tom answered impatiently. "It really interests me!"

"Well, since you insist on it, and since by the fact of your presence here you show your sympathy for my people, I will try to briefly answer your question. I will give you my own non-academic opinion on this matter."

"In the history of mankind," I continued, "one can trace a clear trend: the smaller a nation is, the sooner it disappears from the face of the earth. Even large nations cannot escape this fate. The ancient Egyptians and Babylonians sank into oblivion, of the mighty Assyrians there remain only a few. Hundreds of small peoples disappeared together with their unique cultures. Only one people—the Jewish nation—is alive and well after almost four thousand years of existence. Like a flexible reed, this nation does not break under the storms of history and does not show any sign of perishing no matter what kind of treatment it encounters on its historical path."

"The main guarantee of Jewish survival is the Torah, which laid the modern democratic ideals of social justice and contains appeals for mutual aid and tolerance to all peoples.

The social ideals embodied in the Torah formed the basis of Christianity and Islam as well as modern Western civilization. For Jews, the Torah has been the source of the explanation for the meaning of existence and sanctification of each human life. Another reason Jews have survived, despite the hatred surrounding them, is their attitude toward intellectual activity and spiritual aspirations, which for thousands of years created a favorable atmosphere for human talent to evolve. Other secrets to Jewish survival are the spirit of philanthropy embedded in the Torah—a prescription to help the unfortunate and needy—and the ideals of freedom, which prevent Jews from submitting to alien moral and political authority.

"Armed with such powerful weapons for survival, Jews have never succumbed to the general trend. That Jewish resilience seriously annoyed some of the larger nations among whom the Jews lived. And look at what has happened in our lifetime: after two millennia of exile and persecution, and after the recent destruction of six million Jews, we were able to revive our national home, our country—the State of Israel.

"But let's get back to your question. For centuries, Jews have lived among many different nations, always in groups too small to defend themselves. From the time of antiquity and up to the present, there was never a lack of excuses for blaming them: they were blamed for undue aggressiveness and for passivity, for prudence and for folly, for excessive vindictiveness and for contemptuous cowardice, for intelligence and for stupidity.

"It is a universal human quality to look for scapegoats, to lay the blame at someone else's door. Human hatred exists on many levels: among individuals, inside families, settlements, different ethnic groups, and peoples. For many centuries, Jews have lived in different countries side by side with the local population, doing their best to retain their religion and not to be absorbed and assimilated. From time to time, hatred toward them accumulated and reached the critical point. They became lightning rods for politicians and demagogues, who used hatred toward Jews as a simple means of distraction from responsibility for their own failures and sins. The culmination of that universal hatred was the Holocaust, when the Germans and other people turned into the devil incarnate, creating an industry of mass annihilation of innocent people, including women, children, and the elderly.

"But Jews never gave up. Centuries of persecution, humiliation, and offenses could not crush the Jewish nature; on the contrary, it strengthened and trained it. Jews learned to be steadfast, not to worry about misfortunes, and to continue making their lives worthier, filled with meaning and purpose. Just like an animal that is constantly pursued, Jewish people learned to adjust to practically any conditions and situations. They are indestructible, Tom.

"Such phenomenal adaptability, as I said, causes acute irritation to other people, who apparently believe that this small nation should comply with the universal tendency and inconspicuously disappear like other religious, cultural, and ethnic groups. On top of that, there is also the ever-present envy induced by Jews' disproportionately high achievements in many fields of human activity."

Tom listened with unconcealed interest. Without offering an opinion about what he heard, he impatiently and intently barraged me with other questions: he wanted to know why Jews call themselves the chosen people, why they refuse to believe in Jesus Christ, what they think about original sin, what attitude they have toward Christianity and the coming of the Messiah. He listened to my answers with attention, expressing neither agreement nor disagreement.

"It appears to me," I said to Tom, "you want to allay your own doubts which exist among Christians regarding my people's religion. You do not need to go far. Just read the literature written by the spiritual leaders of your own religious movement. Yesterday, I bought here several books covering those topics. Take my word for it, Jews have never devised any sinister plots against Christians, and they never will. For example, the suspicions that the Jewish Talmud, compiled sixteen centuries ago, contains something derogatory about Christianity can be easily resolved when the text is understood in its historical and circumstantial context. There is a degree of hypocrisy when Christians accuse Jews of not being politically correct fifteen hundred years ago. But who was organizing and participating in the real acts of violence over those entire fifteen hundred years—the Crusades, the Inquisition, expulsions, pogroms, and, finally, the Holocaust? Was it Jews or Christians? We Jews don't have to apologize for our attitude toward Christianity; all we have ever wanted is to exist, to be treated as equals, and to be left alone. Is that too much to ask? By the way, since we are talking about the Talmud, it uses far harsher words and terms when it discusses the consequences of bad behavior by a Jew.

"Of course, there are bad people among the Jews. In this regard, here is what one of the early founders of the State of Israel, Vladimir Zhabotinsky, said. I remember it by heart: 'We are a people as all other peoples; we do not have any intentions to be better than the rest. As one of the first conditions for equality, we demand the right to have our own villains, exactly as other people have them. . .' Once again, Tom, Jews have never had an ideology of hatred toward Christianity or any other religion."

We parted, but a little bit later I started to wonder why Tom was so eager to "inform" me that hatred still exists toward Jews. I decided to find out what the real reason was behind his repeated remarks. Soon the opportunity presented itself.

"Tom," I said, when I happened to run into him again, "you made a special point in letting me know that significant anti-Semitism is still active in this country. Does that mean that, maybe, to some degree, you share similar ideas?"

Tom belonged to the category of people who needed to be asked a direct question about their opinion. Suddenly, maybe for the first time since I met him, a smile came across his strained face.

"No, Vladimir!" he denied firmly, after he had fully digested my question. "Hostility and hatred toward Jews is by no means characteristic of me. I am a straightforward kind of a guy, and if I had any negative feelings towards Jews, I'd tell you about it without hesitation. Judge for yourself: would I have come from Minnesota, at my own expense, would I have spent the days of my short vacation here, if I had been an anti-Semite? I just did not want you to relax and to get the impression that the Golden Age has come for Jews in America."

"Thank you for your concern, but I never had any such illusion!" I responded. "I live in the world of reality and not in the world of dreams. But whatever I am destined to encounter in the future, nothing will ever erase the memory of what I see here now. It is simply incredible. Thanks to the people gathered here, I have acquired a new faith in human beings. For what I have seen here I will always be grateful."

* * *

The next day, during a plenary session, a Christian speaker from CUFI leadership told the audience why the organizers of the summit chose the Book of Ruth from the Bible as a symbol of the inseparable connection between Judaism and Christianity. In this book, a Jewish woman, Naomi, who lived in the country of Moab, lost her husband and two sons. Ruth, a Moabite woman, was the wife of Chileon, one of Naomi's sons. After the death of her family members, Naomi decided to return to her home in the town of Bethlehem in the land of Judea, and she urged Ruth to return to her own mother in Moab. But Ruth categorically refuses to do that, expressing her devotion to Naomi and her people with the unforgettable words that are still uttered at Jewish wedding ceremonies: "Where you go, I will go; where you lodge, I will lodge; your people shall be my people, and your God, my God. Where you die, I will die; and there I will be buried. The Lord do so to me, and more also, if anything but death separates you and me." (Ruth 1:16–17).

"And now, just as Ruth the Moabite," said the presenter, "with a clear conscience, the CUFI organization declares its allegiance to the Jewish people and to the State of Israel, without expectation of any rewards for that manifestation of brotherly love.

"The story of Ruth is interesting, because it does not end with a mere declaration of loyalty. With the blessing of Naomi, Ruth married again and gave birth to a son. This helped Naomi forget about her loneliness, because now she was a happy grandmother. That's not all. Ruth's son was called Obed. Obed became the father of Jesse, and Jesse became the father of David, who was his youngest son, the favorite king of the Israeli people. After many years—as recounted in the New Testament—Jesus, the descendant of David, was born in Bethlehem to the Jewish woman, Mary, wife of the Jewish carpenter, Joseph.

"Without Ruth, Jewish history would not have continued, and the history of Christianity would not have started. In announcing her decision to share the fate of the Jews, Ruth did not expect any rewards either in this world or after death. What is more, she fully realized that by her decision she was making her own life far more complicated. However, Ruth was firm in her determination to follow Naomi and stay loyal to the faith she had linked her fate with. Just like Ruth, guided by unconditional love and not expecting any selfish rewards, Christian Zionists express their firm determination to protect and support Israel. Their motto is the words of Isaiah (62:1): 'For Zion's sake I will not keep silent, for Jerusalem's sake I will not remain quiet, till her righteousness shines out like the dawn, her salvation like a blazing torch.' Christian Zionists understand what seems beyond the grasp of many others. And now, when atheism is trying to destroy religion, and radical Islam is gaining more and more influence, Jews and Christians are faced by the same enemies, and their fates are linked more than ever before. Atrocities of any kind that start with Jews do not end with Jews" [quoted from memory].

* * *

Another unforgettable meeting we had during the summit was with a Chinese American couple, preacher Hong Yang and his wife Esther Yang, who we met by chance. Looking for a secluded corner in the building to rest during the break, we passed by a middle-aged woman sitting at a coffee table. As we sat down opposite her, we introduced ourselves, and soon a conversation started between us. Esther and her husband—he joined us at the very end of the conversation—came from Communist China in the 1980s. Since my wife and I had more than thirty years of experience living in a communist country, we had many things to discuss.

Esther told us about the modern-day slavery of millions of Chinese people who live on a meager salary, about the rampant corruption in China, the unrelenting persecution of Christians, and how the communist government, in search of ever-more income, is mercilessly and irreparably damaging the environment.

The Yangs were born and brought up in Henan Province, not far from Kaifeng, known for its ancient synagogue (now destroyed) dating back to the twelfth century. The family Hong Yang grew up in was not religious, but Hong suffered from spiritual emptiness, which he sought to somehow fill. In search of the answers to his questions, he spent many hours in the local library learning about the universal human values dealt with by such authors as Shakespeare, Milton, Pascal, Hawthorne, Dickens, Tolstoy—which were writers not widely known in China. By the mid 1980s, he managed to meet some American Christian missionaries who came to his town for a visit. After their return to the US, the missionaries wrote to offer him a scholarship at the School of Theology in Cleveland, Tennessee. As strange as it might sound, the communist authorities of the provincial town where Hong lived not only readily gave him permission to study abroad but even expressed hope that the knowledge he would obtain for free in America would help him to build Communist China.

"But how can theology help a godless country?" my wife and I asked at the same time. Esther was expecting our question. She laughed merrily and explained that party members and bureaucrats in China are often uneducated people. In the case of her husband, they decided that "Theological College" was the same as "Technology College." After graduating from college and then theological academy, Hong became a pastor. From that moment he joined the Christian movement supporting the Jewish people. The struggle against anti-Semitism and the attempts at depriving Israel of its legal status were close to Hong and Esther Yang's hearts. They associated the plight of the Jewish people with the merciless persecution of Christians and small ethnic groups they observed in the country where they were born and grew up.

Our meeting with the Hongs developed into a warm friendship.

* * *

Due to growing atheism in America and an increasing number of pro-Palestinian and pro-Islamic students, many colleges and universities in this country have become an arena for anti-Israeli, anti-Semitic, and anti-Christian demonstrations and initiatives, pursuing political goals that have nothing to do with education. This is why it was very encouraging to see at the CUFI Summit the participation of five hundred Christian student delegates representing two hundred different colleges in the US. These young people were actively preparing themselves to confront manifestations of anti-Christianity, anti-Zionism, and anti-Semitism in their schools. The young men and women were dressed conservatively and with good taste, they were respectful and warm, and they demonstrated sincere devotion to their cause.

On the last day of the summit, we visited members of Congress on Capitol Hill. During the visit we had an opportunity to meet three young women, students at the Moody Bible Institute in Chicago. They told us that education there is conducted in a spirit of respect toward the Jewish roots of Christianity. The students showered us with questions about Judaism; a feeling of mistrust towards Judaism was alien to them. In parting, it was our mutual decision that our new friends would spend the next Passover Seder with our family.

On our way back from the summit to Chicago, our seats on the plane happened to be next to two young African-Americans—a young man, originally from Nigeria, and a young woman, born in Congo. We had already met them at the summit as a part of the delegation from Illinois. Large American and Israeli flags, which were handed out at the summit, protruded from their luggage. What a picture!

The summit left an indelible impression on us.

I have no illusions. I understand well that many years will pass before the ugly manifestations of anti-Semitism disappear from the face of the Earth. Even an organization like CUFI with a large number of members pales in comparison with the ocean of hatred toward Jews which exists in many countries of the world and with the wish, expressed by many, to completely destroy Israel together with its inhabitants. But that does not prevent me from my happiness at an incredible miracle and my joy and satisfaction at learning that there are many people in the world who believe in the justice and the truth of what is written in the Torah, who demonstrate their sincere solidarity with the people who faithfully preserved the true words of God.

My generation witnessed many extraordinary events that are destined to enter the annals of history: the Second World War, establishment of the State of Israel, emigration of Jews from the Soviet Union, the fall of the Berlin Wall, and the subsequent collapse of the first communist state in the world.

And here was another revolutionary historic event: I saw Christianity extending its arm to Judaism for a firm and truly friendly handshake. This was done not by separate individuals or a small group but by five thousand delegates who represented fifty million Christians—a powerful movement of people who are guided by noble ecumenical motives.

After twenty centuries of persecution, crusades, Inquisition, pogroms, vile libel, and the culmination of all of that, the tragedy of the Holocaust, which—as Pastor John Hagee writes in his book, *In Defense of Israel*—was committed by "people who were baptized and regularly went to church as Christians," a really epochal event took place: two monotheistic religions were able to find common points of convergence, enabling them to cooperate, respect, and love one another.

And, who knows—maybe the recent "Arab Spring" sooner or later will be followed by an "Arab Summer," and among the distinguished representatives of Islam will be those who can see the logical result of true faith in One God for all mankind: a joining of the efforts of monotheistic religions in the name of what is most important: the assurance of perpetual existence of the human race, *Homo sapiens*, on the one inhabited planet in the infinite Cosmos, for the sake of the glorification of our universal creator.

To my fellow Jews, who might suspect Christian Zionists of a sinister desire to lure them into Christianity and fear that such Christians are "hunting" for their souls, I say that faith in the natural decency of people is part of a normal psyche. I would remind them that, in many cities and towns of the world, Jews from the bottom of their hearts thank and honor those righteous Gentiles who saved Jews from Nazis; and it does not matter whether the Gentile who rescued the life of a Jew was Catholic, Baptist, Evangelist, Muslim, or atheist. The most important thing is that these people treated another human life with awe, as a sacred gift of God. Without such attitude there would be no mankind and no religion!

In the past and even now, in many countries in the world, people do not have a choice in their worship. However, in the free country where we live, all of us can choose the religion we want to practice. Faith has become a matter of free choice, a subject for fair competition in the market of ideas.

There is no one religion on the face of the Earth that possesses the key to the Final Truth. Choice of religion is a question of individual decision.

None of the Christians I met during the summit demonstrated any desire to take my religion away from me. Any Jew with a genuine, firm, and mature belief in the principles of Judaism is able to withstand attempts to change his or her faith.

When the Messiah comes, we'll finally know who was right and who was not so right. Meanwhile, people ought to respect each other for their faith, for what they feel in the depths of their hearts. Naturally, as a Jew, I would like others to follow the covenants of God according to my faith, but in no way do I deny the adherents of other religions their right to seek their own path to Absolute Truth.

* * *

Soon after returning home from the summit, my wife and I went to a Shabbat service in our Orthodox synagogue. I have a long way to go to achieve the same level of knowledge of religious tradition as those Jews who were brought up in Orthodox families and received religious education. For example, I still am not able to fully understand or read fluently the Hebrew text of the Siddur or the Torah, and from time to time I have difficulty following the prayer leader and periodically need to ask questions. However, during this particular religious service I was really comfortable realizing that I was in the right place, in the right time, where the *Shekinah*—the presence of God—invisibly merges with the hearts of those who praise Him and ask Him for help and direction.

Remembering the recent CUFI Summit, I realized once again that if Christians demonstrated such deep respect and, moreover, love toward the Torah and the people who faithfully worshipped it through millennia, then how much more I and every other Jew should be happy and proud to be a part of our ancient religion and of the people who were faithful to it. The ties connecting Jews to their people will only become stronger when they feel really responsible for the honorable earthly mission assigned to them in the Torah: to bring God into the world by their exemplary conduct and by keeping God's commandments, as it is written in Isaiah (42:6): "I the Lord have called thee in righteousness, and have taken hold of thy hand, and kept thee, and set thee for a covenant of the people, for a light of the nations."

According to a very important concept of Judaism, *Tikkum Olam*, religious Jews believe that they are partners with God on Earth in a common mission: improvement of His world. Jews believe that when the world ceases to follow false gods and idols and recognizes the supremacy of God, the world will become perfect.

As someone who grew up imbued with Russian culture, I find it extremely unfortunate that the Russian Orthodox Church, with rare exceptions, in many respects has remained in the Middle Ages in their attitude toward Jews. It has seen Jews not as partners in religious history and belief in the One God but as rivals and enemies. In his article, "Relations between the Russian Orthodox Church and Judaism: Past and Present," Yuri Tabak writes, "For it is only through re-evaluation of the central issues for the Christian: the fate of Israel, the Jewish roots of Christianity, anti-Semitism as the worst sin in the history of Christianity, that the 'crisis of the medieval worldview' (to use Vladimir Soloviev's expression) can be overcome and a decisive step forward in the history of Orthodox-Jewish relations be taken, following in the footsteps of Western Christians."

I have saved for the very end of this chapter another true story that pierced my heart. It happened on the first day of the summit. The last speaker during the plenary session was Dennis Prager, syndicated radio talk-show host, columnist, author, and public speaker. Prager, who is Jewish, at the end of his remarkable speech, which was many times interrupted by bursts of applause, spoke about the suspicions harbored by some in the Jewish community about the true intentions of the Christians toward the Jews.

After paying tribute to the heroic deeds of righteous Gentiles during the Holocaust, Prager said that, even now, when conversing with Christians, he cannot overcome his inner unspoken question: "Will this person hide me from enemies if, God forbid, the Nazis come to power in this country?"

Then the break was announced. Wearing a kippah on my head, which distinguished me from other men, waiting for the next session, I stood leaning against a pillar in the middle of a large hall. Suddenly, I felt a light tapping on my arm. Turning, I saw a petite middle-aged woman wearing a green blouse and a skirt. Judging by the features of her pleasant face, she was most probably Asian. She got to the point without preamble. With a smile I used to see in my childhood on the face of my mother when she caressed me, this woman took my hand in hers and, looking intently in my eyes, uttered these unforgettable words:

"Don't worry," she said, slightly squeezing my arm, "I will hide you!"

I did not know if I should feel exalted because I had the chance to meet another angel in my life, one who looked like an ordinary person, or anxious because once again I was reminded that Jews should always be ready to encounter the ugly face of evil.

IN CONCLUSION

THE EQUATION DESCRIBING the unfathomable mystery of existence of each separate individual and the entire human race on our planet inevitably requires the inclusion of God. Only through faith in the one living God does the temporary, fleeting existence of man on the tiny speck in the universe called planet Earth acquire this tangible meaning that shines in the eyes of those who live with Him in their hearts. The world-renowned scientist Herman Branover says,

> The sole genuinely compelling rationale for preserving for ages to come the priceless gift of learning and knowledge is that abandoning our mission would be intolerable and impossible. This mission was entrusted to us by a higher power, and it requires us to carry the treasures of the spirit over the oceans of spiritual void, to keep the light burning through the all-pervading darkness, to serve God, acknowledging our devotion to Him and our striving to experience His divine presence.
>
> And perhaps there is wisdom in the belief that, for as long as each generation has at least one man carrying the Book of Books in his soul, the endless thread linking the people with its past will never break, and the people will remain indestructible and eternal.

Paraphrasing the famous saying of Mother Teresa, there is nothing greater than to do something beautiful for God.

Every day I come to the synagogue to attend the minyan service where, together with my fellow Jews, I utter prayers to God thanking Him for giving me a human body, the gift of life, and an immortal spirit. Minyan has become an indispensable part of my life, and the synagogue is my home, where I come to start every new day with a conversation with God.

One of the ancient prayers, the *Amidah* prayer, is an integral part of the religious service. If so desired, at the end of this prayer, the worshiper may turn to God with personal requests. For many years, when I said the Amidah prayer, I did my best not to bother God, who is "busy taking care of the entire universe," with my small requests. But the important things that I could not resist asking His help for, things that were vitally important to the future of myself and my family, these humble requests were fulfilled. For me, His answer to my personal prayers is the unsurpassed miracle I experience over and over in my life. To God, who time and time again has bestowed His grace on me, I'll be in debt until my last breath.

CPSIA information can be obtained at www.ICGtesting.com
Printed in the USA
LVOW06*2351091213

364594LV00002B/2/P